CUBA: IT MATTERS

CUBA: IT MATTERS

negotiations in a changing world

Jay S. Brickman
and
Maria Conchita Mendez

ISBN: 1511607769
ISBN 13: 9781511607766
Library of Congress Control Number: 2015905507
CreateSpace Independent Publishing Platform
North Charleston, South Carolina

The opinions, beliefs, and viewpoints expressed by the authors reflect our own personal experience. We have tried to recreate events, locales, and conversations from our memories of them. US-Cuban relations are at a very dynamic state, we have tried to anticipate the changes that may take place. We have made every effort to ensure that the information in this book was correct at press time. Our opinions in no way represent those of our current employers, they are strictly our own.

Contents

Preface vii

Chronology. xiii

Chapter 1 One Conclusion, Two Paths · 1

Chapter 2 From Camagüey to Exile · · · · · · · · · · · · · · · · · 11

Chapter 3 Latin American Journey: from Redneck to Yuma · · · · · · · · 31

Chapter 4 Cuba Matters· 39

Chapter 5 New Dynamics · 45

Chapter 6 Historical Discord· 55

Chapter 7 Miami Mania· 65

Chapter 8 Passion, Persistence, and Patience · · · · · · · · · · · · · · · · 97

Chapter 9 Politics and *Pollos*· 113

Chapter 10 *Y Cuba Que?*· 123

Chapter 11 After the Euphoria · 135

Chapter 12 No Excuses, *Basta Ya*· 147

Appendix 1. Excerpts from History
Will Absolve Me, 1953 153

Appendix 2. The Monroe Doctrine 171

Appendix 3: Laws and Regulations 175

Cuban Refugee Program, 1972 .177

Cuban Democracy Act, 1992 181

Endnotes. 187

Jay Brickman—Bio 203

Maria Conchita Mendez Piedra—Bio 205

Preface

We spent more than two years developing this book to share what our long experience in trade development has taught us about relations between the United States and Cuba. On December 17, 2014, President Barack Obama took actions that we strongly supported to begin changing this relationship. We had recommended many of these actions, and suddenly we were faced with an interesting dilemma: did our book still matter? Clearly some parts did not. We had outlined what we felt the president should do—and he did it. So we sat down and reviewed our draft to decide whether what we had to say still needed airing. Were we now preaching to the choir?

We soon realized we still had much to say. President Obama's actions, while dramatic, are only the beginning of a long and tedious journey to resolve and repair relations between our two nations. For the future of US-Cuban relations, it matters that we get things right. How the two countries progress could set the pattern for US relations with our neighbors in Central America and the Caribbean. This is a complicated process, and we think the account of our journey together helps shed light on how to proceed. Just as the United States is beginning to improve their relations with Cuba, relations with Venezuela are going in the opposite direction. This underlines the importance of learning from the US-Cuban experience. Do we not have something to learn from fifty-six years of difficult relations between the United States and Cuba that might help avoid similar patterns elsewhere? Cuba matters.

Some academics who assessed our manuscript told us that history need not be included—everyone already knows it. We could not disagree more. The history matters. In the United States, we generally have very short memories; in Cuba there is a much more intensive recall of history. This was clearly illustrated at the April 2015 Summit of the Americas in Panama by the comments made by Presidents Castro and Obama. President Castro apologized about his emotional speech concerning the historical relations between the United States and Cuba. President Obama simply said, "The Cold War has been over for a long time, and I am not interested in having battles, frankly, that started before I was born." As relations develop, the United States must keep in mind that, for Cuba, the Cold War will continue until both countries can resolve the long-held prejudices against each other, prejudices that are rooted in history.

We have aimed to respond to the questions people have repeatedly asked us in both the United States and Cuba. Their questions reflect the need to tie a historical overview into the political realities we have seen. It is with this purpose in mind that we recount our own experiences working in Cuba.

We have also been told by political scientists that everyone understands the lobby process and the role that South Florida has played in determining US policy. That simply is not the case. One of the questions we are most often asked is why it has taken so long to move toward resolution of US-Cuban relations. Will these same forces remain obstacles in getting President Obama the congressional support he needs to finish the job? The lack of compelling reasons and the power of what we call Miami Mania have greatly influenced US-Cuban relations. Those dynamics did not suddenly disappear with President Obama's bold 2014 initiative.

We have lived with the intimidation of working in the Cuban American environment. This effect extends even into the academic community, where we expected greater support. In talking with one major university in Florida, we naïvely asked if decision makers felt budgetary considerations were more important than academic freedom, and the answer was blatantly yes. That matters!

One of the biggest challenges ahead involves how the two countries can deal with each other with mutual respect. Can the United States and Cuba work toward open communication and relationship building—the cornerstones for peacekeeping? We discuss that. We have written *Cuba: It Matters* in order to describe our win-win strategies in our personal dealings with Cuba.

Another major challenge the Obama Administration faces is obtaining the backing of the Republican Congress. What will happen with the embargo that is still in place? Is the Helms-Burton Act even constitutional—or the other twenty-plus laws that hinder normal relations? These are questions that President Obama has to address with a Republican Congress that may not want to support his actions.

Will the president have a mandate to change the current policy? What will happen if Ted Cruz or Marco Rubio wins the 2016 elections? The Cuban American leadership in Congress claims that President Obama has betrayed the exile community. Will the old Cuban guard win the fight? Will new economic interest be strong enough to prevail, or will there be a stalemate?

We are sharing our firsthand experiences of how we navigated our way through the complexity of US and Cuban politics and trade policies. We receive numerous calls on a daily basis from people with a wide range of questions, such as: How did you get involved in Cuba? How did you work together on Cuban projects? Why are relations with Cuba so complicated? How have you managed to work in Cuba? What do I need to do to work in Cuba? What will happen now? We hope that our business experience will provide answers to multiple questions. The politics that have arisen out of the animosity between Cuban Americans and Castro provide a bumpy and difficult journey in implementing positive resolution for both countries.

Many of our friends and associates have pressed us to write about this. We replied that there are hundreds, if not thousands, of books about

US-Cuba relations. They countered with a question: how many people do you know who were actually on the ground doing what you two have done? We agreed that there were some, but not too many. We decided to share our background, experience, and analytical ideas regarding the relations between the United States and Cuba.

We are not academics, lawyers, politicians, or diplomats, but between us we have been working in Latin America for decades and have dedicated more than seventy years to working on issues concerning Cuba. You may not agree with our approach and conclusions—quite often, we don't even agree with each other—but we think what we have to say does matter. At this key time, we want to see US-Cuban relations get off to a good start. We want to talk about the lessons learned and the ways to avoid making old mistakes again.

Our journey has been a long one. The road has, by no means, been direct, as you will notice in the text. To those who have supported us, thank you, and to those who continually erect roadblocks that prevent our message from being heard, we support your right to be wrong.

In writing this book, we have been like the perfect storm, our opposite points of view clashing as we strived to show that two countries with different standpoints can normalize relations while, at the same time, maintaining their sovereignty and developing a win-win strategy.

We would like to thank all of those who have contributed to the book. Because of the sensitive subject, we prefer not to name them, but they know they have our deep appreciation. Special thanks to Sally Antrobus, our editor, who guided us.

Maria: I want to thank my Cuban American family, in particular my father, who passed away in 2005, for their unconditional support and for allowing me the freedom to be my own person. My mother refuses to visit Cuba to this day. Her life there was turned upside down and inside out, changing radically from one day to the next. But despite the upheaval in their own lives, my parents gave me the best support in my outspoken ways, even when they did not agree with my views.

Jay: Maria Conchita and I disagree in too many respects to count. Yet we share a driving interest in getting beyond the current situation of policies in neighboring countries that fail to serve either nation well. As a result of this shared interest, while some players remain fixated on differences, we have both become specialists at identifying common ground. Thanks to all those who helped us become so. Special thanks to Charles Silverstein, who in one late-night conversation asked, "Does Cuba matter?"

Chronology

(Adapted from BBC News, "Cuba Timeline: A Chronology of Key Events," 2012, http://news.bbc.co.uk/2/hi/americas/1203355.stm)

1492	Christopher Columbus claims Cuba for Spain.
1607	Havana founded and becomes capital.
1526	Importing African slaves begins.
1762	Havana captured by a British force.
1763	Havana returned to Spain by Treaty of Paris.
1868–78	Ten Years' War of independence ends in a truce, with Spain promising reforms.
1886	Slavery abolished.
1895–98	José Martí leads second war of independence; United States declares war on Spain.
1898	United States defeats Spain, which cedes Cuba to the United States.
1902	Cuba becomes independent, but the Platt Amendment keeps it under the protection of the United States, which retains the right to intervene in Cuba's internal affairs.
1906–9	President Estrada resigns, and the United States occupies Cuban territory, following a rebellion led by José Miguel Gomez.
1909	Gomez becomes president and is soon tarred by corruption.

1912	US forces help put down black protests against discrimination.
1924	Gerardo Machado promotes mining, agriculture, and public works but establishes a brutal dictatorship.
1925	Socialist Party founded.
1933	Machado overthrown by Sergeant Fulgencio Batista.
1934	In the Treaty of Relations, the United States abandons its right to intervene in Cuba's internal affairs, revises Cuba's sugar quota, and changes tariffs to favor Cuba.
1944	Batista succeeded by the civilian Ramon Grau San Martin.
1952	Batista seizes power again and presides over an oppressive and corrupt regime.
1953	Fidel Castro leads an unsuccessful revolt against Batista.
1956	Castro lands in eastern Cuba from Mexico and wages a guerrilla war from the Sierra Maestra Mountains, aided by Ernesto "Che" Guevara.
1958	The United States withdraws military aid to Batista.
1959	Castro's guerrilla army takes Havana, forcing Batista to flee. Castro becomes prime minister, with his brother Raúl as his deputy and Guevara third in command.
1959	Castro takes power.
1960	US businesses in Cuba are nationalized without compensation.
1961	Washington breaks diplomatic relations with Havana and sponsors an abortive invasion by Cuban exiles at the Bay of Pigs; Castro proclaims Cuba a communist state and begins to ally it with the USSR.
1962	Cuban Missile Crisis ignites when, fearing a US invasion, Castro allows the USSR to deploy nuclear missiles on the island. The USSR agrees to remove the missiles in return for withdrawal of US nuclear missiles from Turkey. Organization of American States suspends Cuba.

1965	Cuba's sole political party renamed the Cuban Communist Party.
1972	Cuba becomes a full member of the Soviet-based Council for Mutual Economic Assistance.
1976	Cuban Communist Party approves a new socialist constitution; Castro elected president.
1976–81	Cuba sends troops to Angola and Ethiopia.
1980	The Mariel Boatlift crisis: some 125,000 Cubans, some of them released convicts, flee to the United States.
1991	Collapse of the USSR leaves Cuba without an easy supply of oil; Soviet military advisers leave Cuba.
1993	The United States tightens its embargo; Cuba introduces market reforms to stem deterioration of its economy—legalization of the US dollar, limited individual private enterprise, and transformation of some state farms into cooperatives.
1994	Refugee agreement made between Cuba and the United States whereby the United States agrees to admit twenty thousand Cubans a year in return for Cuba halting the exodus of refugees.
1996	US trade embargo made permanent in response to Cuba's shooting down of two US aircraft operated by Miami-based Cuban exiles.
1998	Pope John Paul II visits Cuba; United States eases restrictions on Cuban Americans sending money to relatives.
1999	The child Elian Gonzalez is picked up off the coast of Florida after a refugee boat capsized; Miami-based Cuban exiles campaign to prevent Elian rejoining his father in Cuba.
2000	Elian allowed to rejoin his father after prolonged court battles; US House of Representatives approves sale of food and medicines to Cuba; Russian President Vladimir Putin visits Cuba and signs accords to boost bilateral ties.

2001	Cuba calls Russia's shutdown of the Lourdes radio-electronic center "a special gift" to US President George W. Bush; the Cuban government requests help following Hurricane Michelle, and the United States exports food to Cuba for the first time in more than forty years.
2002	January: US-held prisoners taken in Afghanistan are flown to Guantanamo Bay for interrogation; Russia's last military base in Cuba closes down.
	April: Diplomatic crisis arises after UN Human Rights Commission criticizes Cuba's record. The resolution is sponsored by Uruguay and supported by many of Cuba's former allies, including Mexico. Uruguay breaks ties with Cuba.
	May: US Undersecretary of State John Bolton accuses Cuba of trying to develop biological weapons and adds the country to Washington's list of "axis of evil" countries; former US president Jimmy Carter makes a goodwill visit—the first US president to visit Cuba since 1959.
	June: National Assembly amends the constitution to make socialist system of government permanent.
2003	March: "Black Spring" crackdown on dissidents draws international condemnation; seventy-five people jailed for terms of up to twenty-eight years; three men who hijacked a ferry to try to reach the United States are executed.
2004	May: US sanctions restrict US-Cuba family visits and cash remittances from expatriates.
	October: President Castro announces ban on transactions in US dollars and imposes 10 percent tax on dollar-peso conversions.
2005	July: Hurricane Dennis causes widespread destruction.
2006	February: Propaganda war in Havana as President Castro unveils a monument that obscures illuminated messages about human rights displayed on the US mission building.

July: Castro undergoes surgery and temporarily hands control to his brother Raúl.

December: Fidel Castro fails to appear at a parade marking the fiftieth anniversary of his return to Cuba from exile.

2007   May: Castro fails to appear at the May-Day parade.

July: Castro fails to appear at Revolution Day celebration.

December: Castro letter read on Cuban TV saying he does not intend to cling to power indefinitely.

2008   February: Raúl Castro takes over as president on February 28, days after Fidel announces his retirement.

May: Bans on private ownership of mobile phones and computers lifted.

June: Plans announced to abandon salary equality, a radical departure from orthodox Marxist principles.

July: Restrictions relaxed on land available to private farmers in an effort to boost food production.

September: Hurricanes Gustav and Ike inflict the worst storm damage in Cuba's recorded history; crops are destroyed, and two hundred thousand people are homeless.

October: State oil company estimates twenty billion barrels in offshore fields (double previous estimates); EU restores ties; ties with Russia revitalized.

2009   March: Leading Fidel-era figures Carlos Lage, cabinet secretary, and Felipe Pérez Roque, foreign minister, resign; first government reshuffle since resignation of Fidel Castro; US Congress votes to lift Bush Administration restrictions on Cuban Americans sending money and visiting Havana.

April: US President Barack Obama says he wants a new beginning with Cuba.

June: Organization of American States lifts 1962 ban on Cuban membership.

2010   May: Wives and mothers of political prisoners are allowed to demonstrate after intervention on their behalf by Jaime Ortega, archbishop of Havana.

July: President Castro frees fifty-two dissidents under a deal brokered by the church and Spain; several go into exile.

September: Radical plans for massive government job cuts to revive the economy; analysts call it the biggest private-sector shift since 1959.

2011   January: President Obama relaxes restrictions on travel to Cuba; Havana says measures do not go far enough.

March: Last two political prisoners detained during 2003 crackdown are released.

April: Communist Party Congress agrees to look into allowing Cuban citizens to travel abroad as tourists.

August: National Assembly approves economic reforms aimed at encouraging private enterprise and reducing state bureaucracy.

November: Cuba passes law allowing individuals to buy and sell private property for first time in fifty years.

December: Release of twenty-five hundred prisoners, including some convicted of political crimes, in an amnesty ahead of a papal visit.

2012   March: Pope Benedict visits, criticizing the US trade embargo on Cuba and calling for greater rights on the island.

April: Cuba marks Good Friday with a public holiday for the first time since 1959.

2013   December: Presidents Obama and Raúl Castro shake hands at Nelson Mandela's funeral.

2014   January 26: The first ship with cargo docks at the new Port of Mariel.

January 27: The Port of Mariel is formally inaugurated, with participation of all Community of Latin American and Caribbean States (CELAC) members.

March 29: New Investment Law.

December 17: President Obama introduces changes to US-Cuba policy.

2015   April 10–11 Presidents Barack Obama and Raúl Castro meet at the Summit of the Americas in Panama.

June 2 The United States formally removes Cuba from its list of state sponsors of terrorism.

1

One Conclusion, Two Paths

As you will have noted, this book has two authors. Between us, we have more than seventy years of experience living and working in Latin America. Combining our experience, we have visited Cuba more than a hundred times and Washington, DC, at least that many.

Circumstances and history have placed us in a unique relationship. Despite very different backgrounds, we often became allies on projects that affected the opening and maintenance of trade from the United States to Cuba.

We have learned that in dealing with US-Cuba relations, *paciencia* is often the refrain; much patience is needed, and that's followed by *no es facil*. It is not easy.

So that it is clear from the beginning, we want to contribute to forming a better relationship between the two countries. We think that "normal" relations between them would be good for both, and we think the time for that to happen is now. Presidents Obama and Castro have taken the first step, which is reflected in the December 17, 2014, White House Paper and the Summit of the Americas in Panama in April 2015.[1]

Overcoming our wildly different backgrounds, we have united in an effort toward transcending the toxic political and economic environment that existed between the United States and Cuba for more than fifty years. As a result, and despite the embargo, billions of dollars of goods have been sold by the United States to Cuba, and our extensive work has greatly contributed to the opening of trade. We have personally experienced how the Cuban population benefits from the limited trade and contact with US visitors. Every week from 2001 through 2013, a Crowley vessel entered the harbor in Havana (as of 2014, the vessels dock at Mariel). The Crowley name in Cuba has become so popular that in one of the Cuban soap operas, they show the vessel as it enters the harbor. Many associate the ship with poultry and other staples from the United States.

Cuba: It Matters is intended to show how improved relations between the United States and Cuba can promote a better economic and political structure in the Americas. The current governments have risen to the occasion and implemented a new US-Cuba policy. When you have differences, open dialogue, respect, and transparency at all times are the key elements in building the foundations to foster better cooperation. Equally important, we have developed social bridges to promote better relations between the two countries. Our approach has been pragmatic—learning from the past while leaving the past behind and moving toward the future.

We have dined with and had open discussions with Fidel Castro Ruz. We have met with numerous senators, congressmen, governors, agricultural commissioners, business associations, and business executives on a personal level. We have maintained open dialogue with the State Department, and most importantly we have been transparent with both sides. In order to add both balance and depth to our account, we also conducted interviews with past and present Cuban government officials with whom we have worked. Much of the resulting information about various issues in US-Cuba relations is presented in dialogue form. Since we both have strong opinions and often do not agree, it was impossible for us to offer a unified interpretation of those conversations. We don't even see eye to eye on how we got together.

Maria: Let me explain how I first met Jay. I was working with the Jacksonville Port Authority and had to organize a trade mission to Mexico for the president of the port and the board of directors. I wanted to make sure everything was perfect. Having just started working for the Jacksonville Port Authority, known as JAXPORT, I didn't know much about the maritime industries. My first day on the job was the first time I'd even seen a vessel up close.

I called my dear friend Mario Villegas in Veracruz, Mexico, because I needed his help coordinating a port tour and setting up appointments for meetings with the officials there. Former governor Jeb Bush was leading the delegation, and I was entrusted with the success of the trip. There was no way I was going to fail.

Before our departure to Mexico City, a coworker informed me that a certain Jay Brickman had called, was extremely upset, and wanted to know who the hell was coordinating the trip. He had instructed my colleague, with a complete disregard for whatever I was doing at the time, that I was to call immediately. *How obnoxious*, I thought.

Jay was, at the time, the vice president for Crowley Liner Service in Mexico, the largest customer of JAXPORT. I had no idea of this as yet and had not met any of the Crowley staff. Keep in mind I had just started my employment at the port, with a background in sales and marketing, and I had zero knowledge of the maritime industry. I debated whether I should call back, evaluating the urgency of the matter. It was one of those chaotic days, and the last thing I needed was to deal with someone in a bad mood. Between other tasks, I pondered that whole morning whether I should pick up the phone.

Deciding I might as well deal with the issue head on and get it over with, I picked up the phone. We agreed to meet at the Presidente Hotel upon my arrival in Mexico City, but I made it clear that I would not change our program. My day had not started as I had expected, and by the time it ended, I never wanted to hear the name Jay Brickman again. Little did I know!

The impression I had was that Jay was an arrogant, self-absorbed know-it-all executive. I had no interest in meeting him; it would take time away from what I was doing. After I reached Mexico City and survived a long cab ride, we met in the hotel lobby. To my surprise, I became more and more impressed with his knowledge as we talked. I don't recollect how it happened, but we started talking about Cuba, and that was when we began to build bridges.

Jay: As usual, Maria's memory is very convenient. What really happened was that a small customs broker in Veracruz, the owner of which was a personal friend of hers, sent an invitation addressed "To Whom It May Concern," inviting Crowley Maritime to attend a cocktail party promoting trade between the Port of Jacksonville and Mexico. We at Crowley were desperately working to establish that trade, and we had two ships calling at the port specifically dedicated to the Jacksonville-Mexico trade.

Given all the work we were doing, I was incredulous that the Port of Jacksonville had sent an invitation to Whom It May Concern, and that was why I called. When I finally met Maria, I found that we disagreed on almost everything, but we had two things in common. We wanted to promote trade and better relations between the United States and Cuba, and we were absolutely certain that Cuba mattered.

Why? Maria Conchita's background reveals the *why* in her case. In mine, I had lived in Latin America for a number of years, had a great interest in Cuba, and had begun traveling there in 1978. After spending a week there, I was convinced that President Jimmy Carter's policy of looking for a normalization of the relationship between the two countries was appropriate. Years later, Pedro Alvarez, former president of the Cuban Chamber of Commerce and Alimport, the Cuban purchasing organization for all items bought from the United States, said to me, "We may not be as good as we think, but we are not as bad as you think we are. We are normal people. Come see for yourself."

Maria on Jay: Jay Brickman is the *gringo* in the equation, better known in Cuba as the *yuma* (a nickname for US citizens). Unlikely as it seems, given his roots in a Jewish-American family that emigrated from Russia in the early twentieth century, Jay has been called the "dean of US-Cuban businessmen."

On December 16, 2001, a Crowley Maritime ship launched from the United States to call on Cuba—the first cargo vessel to make such a trip in more than forty years. In his role as vice president of government services and head of the Cuban service for Crowley, Jay was instrumental in building relationships and developing the legal infrastructure needed to facilitate this first voyage. It was the culmination of more than twenty years of dedicated work.

Black clouds gathered on the horizon in November 2004 when the US government announced a change in the payment terms with Cuba. The changes threatened to end all commercial trade between the two countries. Jay played a key role in coordinating the effort of the US business sectors to obtain cooperation from both the US and Cuban governments to resolve this potential crisis. He continues to manage the liner-shipping service to Cuba and to build commercial and social bridges between the two countries.

Our journey together in our dealings with Cuba began more than fifteen years ago. We could not be more different, seldom agreeing, and yet together we have built numerous bridges in developing trade and better relationships with Cuba.

Jay on Maria: Maria Conchita Mendez Piedra is considered a "worm" in the Cuban sphere; Fidel Castro called the first wave of postrevolution Cuban exiles *gusanos* (worms). Her family was deeply involved in the sugar industry until their departure from Cuba. Her father, Aurelio A. Piedra, was known as one of the top agricultural engineers in the country. Maria was only nine years old when she left her beloved homeland.

Many of her family members have participated in the influential South Florida–Cuban American Society, which has been instrumental in formulating the US policy of the embargo against Cuba, and some of them disapprove of her active role. Maria Conchita has always stood as an outspoken critic of this policy. She has more than thirty years of experience in international business with a focus in Latin America; Cuba, her homeland, is always her true passion.

Maria Conchita has braved threats personally and against her immediate family from members of the so-called Old Guard (their views are discussed in chapter seven), but she continues to fight for her convictions. She has played a key role in promoting trade and lifting travel restrictions between the United States and Cuba. Once trade and travel sanctions were eased during the Clinton Administration and after Hurricane Mitch in 2001, Maria Conchita was able to organize the largest trade delegation to visit Cuba from Florida in modern times. The Florida contingent who attended the US-Cuba International Trade Fair had the unique opportunity to dine with and talk to President Fidel Castro Ruz in an open setting, and Fidel provided enough time for a question-and-answer period.

Maria Conchita tirelessly used her powers of persuasion to overcome reluctance on the part of Alimport to use a Florida port. She convinced Pedro Alvarez, who was president of Alimport at the time, to make a trial shipment from Jacksonville to Cuba.

After relocating from Florida to Alabama, Maria Conchita applied her persistence and experience to helping build Alabama into one of Cuba's top suppliers of poultry and forest products.

Maria Conchita is a traditional conservative Catholic; I am a liberal reformed Jew. She comes from a family involved in the sugar industry, and I come from immigrants who escaped the Russian-Japanese war and settled in Mobile, Alabama, in the segregated Deep South. She grew up with a silver spoon in her mouth and a strong work ethic. Her maternal grandfather, Dr. Pedro Antonio Alvarez Rodriguez, was a prominent attorney who represented the sugar tycoons. I grew up living above my parents' corner grocery; I was stacking cans in the shelves at the age of three.

Maria: I never understood why we left Cuba; in my childish mind, my life was perfect. My world revolved around Morón, where the sugar mill Central Morón was located, near the small city of Pina. Forty-one years would go by before I returned to my homeland. From the day I left, Cuba remained in my heart; I yearned for its fabulous music, rich history, savory foods—and the Malecón, the essence of Cuba, Havana's waterfront esplanade. I could smell and taste the Bay of Havana and see the multiple varieties of palm trees—I'm told there are more than 150 varieties. I nursed my vivid memories of Varadero, el Valle de Yumuri, the Havana Zoo, Manacas, and my grandfather's farm, Doña Charo. Cuba mattered greatly, and it shaped my life.

I have lived in many places, but there is nothing more majestic than the golden sun as it descends in the west, with its magical reflection in the Bay of Havana, the sky lighting up in bright hues of red and orange, and the golden rays slowly disappearing into the horizon just as the birth of the full moon begins reflecting on the calm waters of the bay. It takes your breath away. Cuba is a vital organ that injects life into my very existence. That's my Cuba—*mi Cubita*!

Jay: As Maria Conchita and I developed our professional lives, our paths paralleled one another's for over forty years. We both attended the University of Florida and focused on Latin American studies. We fell in love with the diverse cultures in the Americas, their typical foods, the colorful blend of people, and the gaiety of their music.

For my graduate studies, I attended Johns Hopkins in Washington, DC, and Maria Conchita had just arrived in DC to do an internship with the National Association of Security Dealers. We had both lived in Central America, Venezuela, Miami, and Jacksonville, and we knew a lot of the same people, but we had never met. Ironically, Maria is now residing in Mobile, Alabama, my birthplace, and I am living in Miami, where she began her US journey. It took a while for destiny to bring us together.

We both have a passion for Cuba. I am completely convinced that normal relations between the United States and Cuba would be beneficial for both countries. Maria has always yearned for her homeland and never understood the embargo. She always dreamed of returning to Cuba.

Maria: There are historical differences between the two countries, and there are a number of real and perceived obstacles that have prevented them from simply entering into the relationship that most countries in the world have. Cuba is less than a hundred miles from the US shore. What makes it so controversial? We need to reexamine those controversies. They have led to a number of misconceptions. As an example, who in their right mind really thinks that the Castros can consume all the agricultural products they purchase from the United States?

A group of us traveled to Camagüey, Cuba's third-largest city.[2] In the group was an American who was married to a Cuban American. Before his departure to Cuba, the family had filled his head with numerous fallacies, and he continually commented on how the Cuban people had nothing to eat.

Jay: Maria finally lost her patience, stopped our *bicitaxi* (bike taxi), jumped out, and headed directly to the first home in sight.

Maria: I knocked at the door and explained myself to a bewildered man, who called his wife. He told her that we wanted to come in, check if they had a refrigerator, and then asked if they had any food inside. To the surprise of our American colleague, inside the fridge was a large bag of Tyson chicken legs, among other things.

Jay: After Maria's invasion of this family's home in the middle of the night, they asked the rest of us to come in, and we sat by the dinner table while the lady made coffee for us all. We noted, as our American colleague turned redder and redder, that they had a TV, fan, telephone, stove, etc.

So what has been the key to our success? Both of us are determined in our desire to see change. We are persistent, transparent, respectful, and have had the good fortune to work with organizations that have supported our efforts. We also have a special chemistry and talent for never giving up and always trying to find a path.

Passion has its cost. Maria, while employed by the Jacksonville Port Authority, took the largest delegation to the US-Cuba International Trade Fair, held in November 2001 in Havana. A few months later, because of her stand favoring dialogue toward ending the embargo, she and her family faced serious harassment from Cuban American groups. She resigned and went to work for the Alabama State Port Authority, where support for and commitment to Cuban trade have allowed her a free hand in developing the state's relationship with Cuba.

Maria has experienced a tremendous amount of conflict and some threats against her life; in my case, I have experienced a corporate cost. In spite of opening up new markets and promoting substantial growth in other areas in the Americas, I became stereotyped as "that guy who works on Cuba." After a bumpy start, we have seen the trade grow to millions of tons of agricultural goods and hundreds of vessel calls. More importantly, we have seen relations between the two countries improve. I would not change a thing.

Cuba is a small country, yet it has cast a very long shadow over US relations in Latin America. Presidents Obama and Castro's new policy will establish better relations between the United States and Cuba, and that relationship can greatly improve the development of a more dynamic inter-American system to participate in the world of global competition for trade and ideology.

To understand the second generation of Cuban Americans better, the children of the first wave of Cuban exiles, we turn now to Camagüey.

2

From Camagüey to Exile

MARIA CONCHITA MENDEZ

My recollections represent the journey of many in my generation who left Cuba as children in the early 1960s. We have distinct memories and a never-ending yearning for our homeland. For us, Cuba definitely matters a great deal.

I was born in Havana one hot summer night in mid-August. A few weeks after my birth, my parents transported me to the sugar-growing complex that would be my home until the day I left Cuba. I grew up pampered and without a care at Central Morón, the largest sugar mill on the island—my own paradise near the village of Pina. It was a world of sugar. During the harvest time, the burned cane was placed in rail wagons as the locomotive moved the wagons to the mill. The air was filled with the smell of molasses. I loved entering the mill with my dad and tasting the *guarapo*, the fresh juice from the cane.

When the cane fields were burned and cinders floated down, I reveled in blackening my skin with the ashes until I was dirty from head to toe and almost as black as the children in the *batey* where the sugar-mill workers lived. It drove my *tata* (nanny) Nancy crazy. Nancy came running from the house shouting, "Look at you. I will never figure out how you manage to get so dirty in so few minutes." She escorted me to the bathroom, placed me in a huge white porcelain tub, and rubbed my skin with blue soap until I was as red as a lobster and my coat of soot had been washed down the drain. She sprinkled me with talcum powder and poured violet water in my hair before combing it.

My father was tall and extremely handsome. His best feature being his piercing dark eyes, eyes that spoke. Everyone called him by his nickname, Yeyo. My mother, always by his side, was a rare beauty. She had curly pale blond hair and a fair complexion and was often called *la gringa*, even though she was 100 percent Cuban.

Besides my parents, brothers, and sister, our home also contained the *tata*, cook, gardener, chauffeur, and a woman who did the laundry on weekdays. It had not dawned on me, of course, that I was spoiled and belonged to the privileged class. We were completely blind to the poverty in the *batey*. To this day, much of Cuba's former upper-middle class has never acknowledged that everything was not perfect, and poverty was rampant. The country had a high illiteracy rate, and thousands of people went to bed hungry. I have met many professionals in Cuba in my age group who are quick to acknowledge that they got their education thanks to the revolution; because they dwelt in poverty, a university education would otherwise have been nearly impossible.

When I was around three, my dad arrived home driving his Jeep, his white Panama hat on top of his jet-black hair, and his boots were covered with thick brown mud as he got out of the vehicle and walked toward the front door. One look from his ebony eyes was enough to stop me in my grubby tracks as I played with one of our pets. He picked me up in his muscular arms to deliver a big hug, plant a kiss on my cheek, and say, "Conchi, young ladies are supposed to be delicate and refined." *Fina y delicada*. To this day, what my daughters remember best about their grandfather are those words.

As our family grew and my brothers and sisters arrived, I had some competition. I was the oldest. My dad took me by the hand and told me the story of how he found me discarded in a garbage can by the side of the road. My brothers and sisters had blond hair, fair skin, and light eyes. They looked like albinos; I was all the opposite, with dark hair and complexion—the black sheep of the family. As I pondered the garbage can, my dad burst out laughing and said, "Sweetheart, you are exactly like me. My spitting image."

I adored my father, even though we often argued. My mother said that was because we were so similar in character—strong-willed and stubborn; some called me the rebel in the family. Dad always said, "In life, it is better to turn red once than yellow fifty times."

Being direct and to-the-point and always expressing myself led me into lots of trouble. As time went by, I slowly learned to be more diplomatic. From my dad I learned the value of hard work, the importance of an education, and to be persistent—to know what I wanted, to never give up, and to fight for my convictions—and most of all, I learned about the love of family. I treasure the love my parents had for each other. In short, I lived in a securely loving home and grew up a free spirit. I had everything. I was spoiled rotten.

Sundays were special. We wore our best clothes. The dresses I remember were made of organza, with lace and a large bow in the back. My hair was combed into a ponytail and fastened with a bow the same color as the dress. The shoes always had to be white, with white socks—perfect for getting messy in puddles. I loved to jump in all the puddles on my path and splatter mud around. How I hated those dresses that my mom bought every year at El Encanto department store in Havana.[1]

On Saturday, our cook, Victoria, began the preparations for Sunday's dinner—a traditional weekly feast. She took one of the chickens from the courtyard and killed it. After she finished plucking the bird, she placed it on a cutting board and cut it into eight pieces. These she placed in a large bowl for the seasoning process. In went sour oranges, garlic, onions, oregano, and other spices, and the covered bowl went into the refrigerator to marinate overnight.

On Sunday mornings, our family traditionally walked to the small Catholic church inside the sugar-mill compound, and other families walked to the Protestant church. Years later, my mom told me that one of the families with whom my parents were friendly was also closely connected to Mario and Lincoln Díaz-Balart, both destined to later become Florida congressmen.

I was always looking for Ernestico. We were inseparable, and at the age of five I was madly in love with him. He was a *chaparrito* (diminutive person)—I was a full head taller. As young children, we once took out a rowboat on the nearby lake, Laguna de la Leche. We swam and talked about the last *Rin Tin Tin* or *Roy Rogers* episode. Our impression of the United States at the time was that it was the land of the cowboys and Indians. Only in Cuba did you have cars and nice houses.

After Mass, Father Guzmán often joined us for lunch. As Papi opened the door of the house, the aroma of *sofrito* wafted out.[2] Victoria liked to pour a bottle of beer on the rice. She had the custom of leaving a little beer in the bottle and sipping it as she cooked. My love for cooking began at an early age, and I still routinely cook with beer or wine, making sure to save just enough to sip as I prepare the meal.

Christmas was the most memorable time. How I loved *la Navidad*. If I prayed hard, I thought we might get snow on Christmas Eve. Our home was always visited by Santa Claus and *los reyes magos*, the three kings. I had no idea that some children did not receive a single present during this joyous season or that poverty was prevalent in Cuba.

We usually traveled to Havana to celebrate *la Noche Buena*—Christmas Eve—and New Year's. We stayed in El Vedado at the home of my maternal grandparents, *Abuelo* Pedro Antonio Alvarez and *Abuela* Tete. They complained about our wild behavior. According to our grandparents, anyone who was not from Havana was a *guajiro* (country bumpkin). Today, I must agree that we were undisciplined, particularly when my brother Aurelio and my cousin Tessie got together.

How I loved Christmas: all the magical decorations, all the cooking that took place in my grandmother's kitchen, the anticipation of eating *los turrones* from Spain, the smells of *puerco asado* and *mojito* that engulfed the house.[3] The memories live in my heart forever, and I have aimed to pass those family traditions to my daughters and grandchildren.

My uncle Tony, my mother's brother, gathered all of us cousins with great excitement to decorate the Christmas tree. The tree was a huge pine that came from abroad, most likely the United States or Canada. We stood quietly and watched with sheer joy as Uncle Tony arrived with the chauffeur and brought the tree into the house.

On one wall of the living room was a large nativity built out of different-sized boxes covered with crushed-brown paper. We reconstructed ancient villages, rivers, lakes, and the journey of Mary and Joseph to Bethlehem. Once we completed all the scenery, we carefully placed the delicate glass figurines of houses, animals, grass, trees, and the cast of the nativity.

On Christmas Eve, my cousins and I were filled with anticipation and on our best behavior. My aunt Rosy assembled us on the patio to practice Christmas carols to sing to our parents that evening. We also presented a play, each of us dressed up as a character and memorizing our lines; the youngest child always played baby Jesus.

The cook prepared a spectacular meal for Christmas Eve. My grandparents' home was one of the few in Havana that had central air-conditioning back in the 1950s. The cook lowered the thermostat to fifty degrees as she started to marinate a pig; this was done the night before. Christmas Eve morning while the marinated pig roasted in the backyard, the cook made *congri* (Cuban black beans and rice) and prepared *yuca* (cassava) with *mojo* sauce. We ate similar meals the rest of the year, but what was special about this was that the roasting of the whole pig brought families together to play dominoes and share stories while waiting eight hours or so for it to cook.

After dinner, Dad sat with us on the patio to check if we could see Santa Claus approaching with his sleigh. We put out hay for Santa's reindeer; after such a long journey they had to be terribly hungry. I retired to bed praying for forgiveness for all my antics, terrified of getting nothing in the morning but a box full of coals.

New Year was another big celebration; again we ate roast pork, rice and black beans, and cassava. The adults danced to the sounds of Benny More and drank cider from Spain. I think I was around six when I first heard the name Batista. My uncle was in college, and as we welcomed the new year of 1958, he started talking about the university students Batista had ordered assassinated.

That summer, the Piedras, my dad's side of the family, vacationed together for the last time in Varadero. With more than twenty kilometers of crystal-white sandy beaches, Varadero was among the finest beach-resort areas in the Caribbean and was Cuba's premier destination. During the summer, we stayed in a family home in the DuPont subdivision in front of the most famous beach in Cuba. I can still feel the ocean breeze in my face as I gazed at the transparent aqua waters from horseback, not knowing that I would never return. The memory of that summer has made it impossible for me to return to Varadero. Our plane did stop there once; I think President Hugo Chavez of Venezuela was landing nearby, and all commercial aircraft was redirected to Varadero, but I remained in the waiting area.

I adored my paternal grandmother Mimi, who would take me on her lap as she narrated all kinds of tales about princesses; I try to do the same with my grandchildren. We competed at water sports. My brother Aurelio, knowing I was afraid of crabs, chased me all over the beach with a crab in his hand. We must have been around thirty cousins altogether, of whom my particular buddies were Margarita and Juaco. We reunited at the University of Florida as undergraduates and shared an apartment. Years have gone by, but whenever we meet, it's as though we've never been apart, and we sink cozily back into that special bond of *mi familia*.

Early in the morning at Varadero, I was always on the lookout for the milkman, who drove a black Ford truck. He delivered little glass bottles of chocolate milk. I don't know if it was because of the glass bottle, but I have never tasted creamier chocolate milk. On the beach, the air smelled of freshly roasted peanuts that vendors wrapped in paper bundles called *cappuccinos*, and on the radio we heard the song *Manicero* (Peanut Man). I walked in the sand, dancing to the music, and I still love to dance.

It was at Varadero that I overheard my uncles talking about the deplorable situation in Havana. How bombs and gunfire were going off all day long. No one was safe; every day, a dead body appeared, and people avoided going out in the evening for fear of not returning. I thought the adults were exaggerating, but sadly, we never met again for a family gathering in Varadero or anywhere else in Cuba. My father died without ever going back, although he relived some of his days in Cuba from my travels to the island, particularly when I visited Pina and the sugar mill.

I was seven when I first became conscious of the reality of poverty. My *tata*, Nancy, took me to her home one day. It was a deplorable place in the tenement housing on the outskirts of the sugar-mill complex. The house was a *bohio*, a small hut of no more than ten by ten feet, with a dirt floor and about five old twin-bed mattresses on the floor, stacked neatly in a corner, one on top of the other. As I entered, I saw a skinny little girl sitting on a mat made from palm-tree leaves. I started talking to her. She was clutching an old, dirty rag doll, her most cherished possession. She was barefoot and wearing only panties. I had never seen an image like the one in front of me.

I never forgot her large eyes, brown and sad, as she looked at my doll. I was carrying a doll named Cachucha—the latest trendy toy at the time. My dad had gone to Havana and purchased it as a surprise. At that moment, I grasped that not all children had the same privileges I enjoyed. I had a room full of dolls and toys of all kinds, not to mention board games, a bicycle, skates, and storybooks. A sudden impulse took over, and I gave her my Cachucha doll. She grabbed me tightly, giving me a big hug and a kiss before she ran away to show her mother. At some level, I suppose, I was responding to a sense of the unfairness of life. After that day, I could get away with murder; I think I became my *tata*'s favorite.

Fidel Castro had painted a picture of Cuba's landscape of social injustice in his now famous *History Will Absolve Me* speech, delivered in court in his own defense in 1953. He provided a series of numbers.

Eighty-five percent of the small farmers in Cuba pay rent and live under constant threat of being evicted from the land they till. More than half of our most productive land is in the hands of foreigners. In Oriente, the largest province, the lands of the United Fruit Company and the West Indian Company link the northern and southern coasts. There are two hundred thousand peasant families who do not have a single acre of land to till to provide food for their starving children. On the other hand, nearly three hundred thousand caballerías *of cultivable land owned by powerful interests remain uncultivated. If Cuba is above all an agricultural state, if its population is largely rural, if the city depends on these rural areas, if the people from our countryside won our war of independence, if our nation's greatness and prosperity depend on a healthy and vigorous rural population that loves the land and knows how to work it, if this population depends on a state that protects and guides it, then how can the present state of affairs be allowed to continue?*

Except for a few food, lumber, and textile industries, Cuba continues to be primarily a producer of raw materials. We export sugar to import candy, we export hides to import shoes, we export iron to import plows... Everyone agrees with the urgent need to industrialize the nation, that we need steel industries, paper and chemical industries, that we must improve our cattle and grain production, the technology and processing in our food industry in order to defend ourselves against the ruinous competition from Europe...But...the state sits back with its arms crossed, and industrialization can wait forever.

Just as serious or even worse is the housing problem. There are two hundred thousand huts and hovels in Cuba; four hundred thousand families in the countryside and in the cities live cramped in huts and tenements without even the minimum sanitary requirements; two million two hundred thousand of our urban population pay rents, which absorb between one fifth and one third of their incomes; and two million eight hundred thousand of our rural and suburban population lack electricity.[4]

I lived in a sugar-mill community where sugar was grown for export, and now I had personally encountered something of what the housing crisis looked like for poor people (see appendix 1 for further excerpts from the speech).

We gathered in Havana at the end of that year to welcome the dawn of 1959 with my mother's side of the family. I remember the euphoria people felt thinking that Batista would soon be defeated. In the city, we heard gunshots and explosions, especially in the evenings. All I wanted was to go back to the comforts of my home in Morón. I loved the open sugarcane fields. Even today, if I close my eyes, I clearly remember how my life began to disintegrate with the welcoming of the New Year when I was seven.

The years 1958 and 1959 were challenging. When my parents did not want us to hear their concerned conversations, they spoke in English, and I immediately knew something was wrong. I tried to pick up a word here and there to find out what was happening. Havana was not a safe place, and neither were most other cities in Cuba. My parents spoke of the rebel forces in the Sierra Maestra, the mountain range from which Castro launched the revolution. After he landed in Playa las Coloradas on board the *Granma*, the revolutionaries spread through the mountain range, and with the help of peasant sympathizers, the guerrilla movement was born to combat the Batista regime.

In the evening, my mom and dad sat in their bedroom listening to a shortwave radio. They spoke in whispers, while the static from the radio drove me nuts. I heard them talking softly about what was happening; they did not sympathize with Batista. Mom and Dad were afraid that at any moment, the militia could hide in the cane fields, and all hell would break loose.

I felt so nationalistic during this time. Finally someone was going to bring down the Batista regime. In the early afternoon, I had the habit of walking to a little *bodega* (store) to buy candy. In one corner of the store, I saw an issue of the magazine *Bohemia* that showed pictures of torture conducted by Batista's military. Those images became embedded in my young mind.

Life at the sugar mill continued at its own slow pace, although the *campesinos* (peasants) spoke of the revolutionary forces. "They are getting closer," people said. One evening, my dad gathered us all, and his demeanor was serious. In a grave tone, he explained to us that we could not go outside our compound. The rebel forces had begun descending from the mountains into the countryside, and gunshots could be heard in the distance.

In late December, we departed on our customary eight-hour trip to Havana in my dad's new Oldsmobile. I couldn't contain the urge to start the Christmas preparations, see my cousins, and have some normality back in our lives. As Dad placed our bags in the trunk of the car, he asked us in a low voice to be on our best behavior. One look into his eyes, and I knew he meant business.

The trip to Havana took forever. Every fifty to sixty miles, Batista's military forces, machine guns in hand, manned checkpoints along the main highway. They wanted to know where we were going—every detail of our trip and our final destination. At one of the stops, my dad said to my mom in English, "Batista's days are numbered." Somehow, I understood the phrase.

I was not aware of the political situation, much less what was happening in the country. All I knew was that Fulgencio Batista was regarded as a bad man, and I felt as if I were in jail because I had to remain on our property, and I had seen those horrific pictures in *Bohemia*. The only other political tinge in my awareness was that once, as we walked to church, I overheard women gossip that Batista had been denied entry into the Havana Yacht Club because he was mulatto.

Finally we reached my grandparents' home in El Vedado. The atmosphere was tense, and all the adults spoke in whispers. The festivities on Christmas Eve in 1958 were subdued. For the first time, we did not attend midnight Mass. I was devastated, feeling that my parents, my family, and I were committing a grave, mortal sin. For sure we would all go to hell; the indulgence or good deeds I had been saving would not help me when I met with my Maker.[5] Attending midnight Mass was a tradition in the majority of Cuban households. It was customary for the priest to pick up baby Jesus from the manger at the end of Mass. The children got up from their pews and filed by to give baby Jesus a kiss, as one of the nuns sang *Silent Night* in the small choir box. As I went to sleep that night, I heard shots in the distance, and it seemed quite likely that, because of the fighting, Santa might simply bypass Cuba.

As the family prepared to celebrate the New Year, my cousins and I were given the task of placing twelve grapes in little baskets. The tradition was to eat the grapes at midnight, one for each month, representing good luck and fortune in the welcoming of the New Year. Another tradition was writing down all the bad things that had taken place through the year on little notes and placing these in a bucket of water so that the old year would take them with it. I think I wrote about twenty notes. The custom was to throw the bucket of water onto the street at exactly twelve midnight.

As the final midnight of 1958 approached, all the lights went off in our neighborhood and in most of Havana. We searched for candles. When someone called out, "Happy New Year," we kissed and hugged one another. As we threw the bucket of water out the window, the neighbors in the street chanted, "*Viva la revolución! Viva Fidel!*"

The following day we rapidly returned to Morón. I still recall my dad's worried look as he said with great apprehension, "Finally, Batista has left." Dad was a cautious man, and I heard him talking to mom about the uncertainties of the future. Revolutionaries appeared in every city; people sang and danced in the streets. Fidel was our hero.

I don't remember who gave me a Camilo Cienfuegos doll. He was one of the heroes of the revolution and so handsome that I developed a crush on him, as had every other female. He was scheduled to visit Camagüey soon. I was hoping he would come to the sugar mill. But one evening, as my parents listened to the radio, a bulletin was issued that the Cessna plane transporting Camilo had mysteriously disappeared over the ocean.

I was wide awake all night. Camilo's body was never found. All over Cuba, the people prayed, and later mourned, for the handsome revolutionary. Over the years, some have attributed his death to Fidel, but historians say it really was an accident. Several days later, Fidel officially declared Camilo dead. With tears in my eyes, I gently placed my Camilo doll in a shoe box, while Ernestico, pretending to be a priest, administered last rites. We buried the hero in the back yard, and Ernestico offered more prayers.

Fidel appointed Manuel Urrutia Lléo as president, but he resigned just months later. In July 1959, Osvaldo Dorticos Torrado was appointed president. My grandfather on my mother's side, Pedro A. Alvarez, summoned us to Havana, saying, "We all need to meet as soon as possible. This is a command." We departed for Havana.

Dorticos, the new president, was my mother's cousin. During his college years, he lived at my grandparents' home while attending law school at the University of Havana. In Cuba during that period, as well as under Batista, the university was the cradle for political parties. Dorticos had joined the university's Communist Party and participated actively. Declaring that he refused "to have a communist living under his roof," my grandfather kicked Dorticos out of the house. Although my grandfather continued paying for his university and living expenses until he graduated, they otherwise had no more contact.

My mother's father had grave reservations about the future of Cuba after Dorticos was appointed president. When my parents arrived at the meeting, my grandfather kept reiterating, "*Esto es comunismo.*" *This is communism.*

He informed the family that we must leave Cuba and go to Miami. No way was I going to go; my place was in Cuba. Dad informed his father in-law that he was not going. What a relief, I thought—we were not leaving. I remember them arguing. As the tone of their voices grew more intense, I was proud of my dad. No one was going to control his family, even though my grandfather was the patriarch, who expected to be obeyed.

Then one morning the rebel forces entered our house. As they ran into our kitchen and ransacked the pantry, they seized all the food and shouted at my mom, "*Gringa*, now is the time for your children to go hungry."

I had rarely seen my mom get so upset or angry. With all her valor, she said, "I am as much a Cuban as you, and it's time that no child goes hungry in Cuba."

During this period, food became scarcer and scarcer. Signs in the countryside, as well as most major cities, read, "*Gringo*, go home."

The following day, my dad showed up with a new pet, a goat that was only three days old. Aurelio named her Pintica. The goat followed Aurelio and me all over the sugar mill, and because she was still so young, we took turns feeding her with one of the small toy bottles I had for my dolls. How we loved her. Our *tata* fussed at us not to bring the goat inside the house, but of course we didn't listen. One day, Pintica ate my father's newspaper before he had seen it. As she grew, she became a handful, eating our neighbors' flowers and destroying all manner of things. Then she developed horns and began chasing our *tata* around the yard.

One day when we got home from school, Pintica had disappeared; there was absolutely no sign of her—not the merest clue. My brother and I searched the whole neighborhood, calling out for her. I had tears in my eyes; I kept thinking the worst. When my dad arrived from work he helped look for Pintica, promising to resume helping us search at daybreak.

Yet he seemed very calm, which led me to suspect that he knew more than he was telling. We sat down for dinner that night to find that our cook Victoria had prepared goat stew. My brother and I accused her of killing our beloved goat—she was a murderer! No one ate even a morsel of the stew that night. Indeed, Pintica had been slaughtered. Years later, we learned that our dad authorized the killing because of the food shortages. I have never eaten goat again.

Father Guzmán visited us more often; he urged my parents to get us out of Cuba. It was rumored that Fidel was going to take children from their parents and send them to Russia. The project to get children safely out of Cuba, run by the Catholic Church and in conjuncction with the CIA, was known as the Peter Pan plan. More than forty thousand children of all ages were taken from their parents and sent to the United States. Some went to live temporarily with families, others never saw their parents again, and many were placed in orphanages. Mom confronted Dad only very few times in her life, and this was one of them. She was adamant: we would either depart together, or we would all stay in Cuba. I hated seeing my parents argue. They concluded that it was time we joined the rest of our family in Miami.

Every night before we retired to bed, our parents sat us down and warned us to make sure we did not repeat to anyone outside the home a word of what they said in the house. By this time, we had an appointed government official on every block who reported all the activities of his neighbors, and my parents feared being sent to jail at the whim of an official.

As the summer of 1961 approached, our little family was the only portion of our extended family still in Cuba. That summer, we didn't go on our usual vacation but stayed at the mill. How I missed my cousins and our big family reunion. A sense of insecurity took over my life. My parents had to solve the problem of our education; they didn't want us to be indoctrinated by the government. All my life, I attended Catholic all-girls schools. The nuns in their spooky black medieval habits played an important role in my upbringing. They taught love for humanity, the importance of good deeds, art, literature, piano, embroidery, and theater—everything needed to be the perfect wife. As the sisters often said, "You have to learn to be prim and proper for a nice young man."

But now all the religious orders had been expelled from Cuba. Most of the nuns and priests came from Spain, and they had too often compared the revolution with the Spanish Civil War, during which many children disappeared and were taken to Russia. I felt bewildered; all my aunts, uncles, and cousins from both sides of the family had departed to Miami. A sense of uncertainty and panic developed. As an adult I have suffered from panic attacks, and this was probably their origin.

Castro's government seized businesses and residences. We heard that my grandparents' home had been nationalized, and numerous families had swarmed the house. The same thing happened to other family members and friends. Word got out that the government would not allow professionals to leave Cuba. My dad was an expert in sugar production; Cuba was the largest producer and exporter of sugar in the world. Dad was one of the top agricultural engineers in the country by this time and being recognized around the world. My mother was afraid the government would take her children away and that we would not be allowed to leave Cuba together as a family.

Around August 1, 1961, late in the evening, Dr. Venegas, our family physician, frantically knocked at our front door. He was extremely agitated and out of breath as he asked to talk to dad immediately. As my dad came into the living room, the doctor said, "Yeyo, you have to leave Cuba within twenty-four hours."

What was so urgent that we had to go? The doctor explained that earlier in the day he had tended to a revolutionary agent who died in a car accident on the main highway, and inside the man's jacket was an arrest warrant for my dad.

That evening will always be engraved in my mind. My dad asked our maids to pack one suitcase for each of us. I was paralyzed with fear. Dad told us we could each take just one small toy with us on the trip. I had a meltdown because my favorite doll was three feet tall. A replica of Princess Ann, it was a gift from my godfather, who had bought it in England. I would have to choose another. My parents gave Nancy and Victoria all our valuables to hide. They were crying, and I was having a tantrum and refused to get into the car. This was one of the few times that my dad spanked me; there was no way I would win this battle.

My parents loaded the car in silence, their eyes revealing tremendous sadness. Dad told us that if by any chance we were pulled over, we were to keep still and very quiet. He tenderly laid us on the floor of the car and covered us with a blanket. My father was thirty-six years old, and my mom was thirty-two. Later in life, I could visualize how hard it must have been to leave behind the world they knew, all their possessions, the home they loved, and depart for a foreign country with four young children and a fifth on the way. I was nine, Aurelio eight, Maggie six, and Tony five. I have asked myself numerous times if I would have had the courage to turn my back on everything and walk away.

We arrived in Havana, Dad having driven all night, and proceeded to my aunt's house in Miramar. She had already left Cuba, and the house was so quiet. At any minute I expected to see one of my cousins appear and surprise me.

A powerful force overcame me as I sat by the window trying to capture every image. *Mi Cuba*. My Cuba. Through the window, I could see the walls of the Colegio La Imaculada, an all-girls Catholic school. That evening a doctor came by and gave us each the smallpox vaccine. It caused a terrible reaction, and I developed a high fever. My arm itched, and an ugly blister developed.

As evening came, we were famished, and there was nothing to eat. The mango and banana trees had no fruit. Dad went out to see what food he could find. Sometime later, he returned with some tiny chicken drumsticks; he told us the chickens in Cuba had nothing to eat either, and that was why the drumsticks were so small and skinny. Years later in exile, Dad revealed to us that we ate frog legs that night.

The Panamanian ambassador was a dear friend of the family. My dad called her early in the morning, and she sent the embassy chauffeur to pick us up. Upon our arrival at the embassy, we kids dashed into the pool as the adults talked. It was a relief to be able to play for a short while.

Back in the living room of my aunt's home that evening, with the lights off to avoid attracting attention, Dad told us the story of how he and Mom met as children. They were neighbors. When mom was three years old, he told her that someday he would marry her. My mom became my dad's sweetheart at the age of thirteen, and they dated for eight years before getting married on November 20, 1950.

Mami asked us to pray the rosary; I knew something was not right; the atmosphere in the room was that of a funeral. I could not comprehend what was happening. As we finished praying, Dad asked us to obey Mom in everything she asked and revealed to us that, in the morning, he would be leaving Cuba.

For the first time in my life, I could not speak. My stomach was in knots. My father was leaving us. What was happening to my family? On August 9, 1961, early in the morning, my dad departed to Miami with the ambassador, posing as her lover. The following day, the embassy sent a car to take us to the airport. Mom instructed us that if the authorities asked us about Dad, we had to inform them that our parents were getting a divorce. My parents always got along so well that we scarcely grasped what she meant by a divorce.

Mami had always depended on Dad, but on August 10, 1961, she was determined to leave Cuba. As we arrived in the airport, the officials were waiting for us and took us to a small interrogation room. Keep in mind this portrait: a young woman of thirty-two, four months pregnant, with four small children, telling the officers that she had no idea where my dad was and that the reason he wanted a divorce was because she was pregnant. They checked our luggage, and it seemed an eternity until the authorities let us go, and we heard the intercom announcement of a Pan Am flight bound for Miami.

That day I left my beloved Cuba, my homeland, the country where I was born, and headed with the rest of my family to Miami. I had no knowledge of what awaited us. I was leaving the safety of my home. I didn't want to leave. I was starting a new life not knowing the language. Forty-two years would go by before I returned to my beloved Cuba.

As the plane began its descent into a strange land, I peered through the window and watched Miami grow closer and closer. The flight was less than one hour. I kept thinking this must be a painful nightmare, and I would wake up in the comfort of my home with my *tata* fussing over me. As the plane made its final approach, Miami looked like a small town compared to Havana.

It seemed a long time before the customs official stamped our Cuban passports and let us proceed. As we reached the exit, I saw my father's silhouette—he had not departed forever with another woman. We embraced in tears and laughter. The most important thing was that our family was reunited.

We took a taxi to my grandfather's apartment on Venetian Way in Miami Beach. According to my father, this was only temporary. Soon we would all return to Cuba. They were so wrong. My grandparents, aunts, uncles, and dad passed away without returning, and my mom, now in her eighties, refuses to visit Cuba.

When the Christmas holidays came, I hoped that Santa and the three kings would bring me all the toys I wanted, because, given our rapid departure, my toys had been left behind. To my surprise, my dad told me Santa and the three kings would deliver the toys to our home in Cuba, and they would leave me one gift here in Miami. I looked him straight in the eye and asked, "If Santa and the three kings are delivering my toys at our home in Cuba, then Fidel cannot be that bad. Let's go back to Cuba." At that time, if I possibly could have, I would have returned to the security I had left behind.

We all lived in my grandfather's apartment. I have spent a lifetime trying to block the painful memories, the tears, at seeing my parents' spirits crumble. My grandfather was always punishing us, and it seemed he was always quarreling about something. My mom's health deteriorated. With no domestic help, she slowly sank into a serious breakdown that lasted more than a year.

After two months in Miami, we departed for Lakeland, Florida, where my mom's sister Teteita lived. The first year was a difficult, horrible year. My sister Issy was born, and my other sister, Maggie, and I looked after her. My mom cried all the time. What had happened to the mother we knew? I hated Lakeland and the nuns at St. Joseph School. They made fun of the way we talked and blamed us for the missile crisis. I had no friends. And then to top everything else, my grandparents moved in with us.

As I turned eleven, I wondered what was happening to my parents. We faced the frustration of not knowing the language, and we were adapting to a completely different culture in direct conflict with my parents' values. I was lost. My story is the story of the many children who left Cuba and whose lives were never the same. I was not a Peter Pan child, but the effects of what happened to me felt much the same as for them. My parents moved to the Abaco Islands in the Bahamas and lived there until the summer of 1972. As a result, I was shipped out to an all-girls boarding school, Holy Name Academy in Tampa, from which I was expelled, and then Rosarian Academy in Palm Beach, where I cultivated lifelong friendships and graduated in 1970.

But I had lost my home forever. I developed a long resentment toward my parents after they dropped me in a boarding school for the first time. I remember lying in bed one evening, crying uncontrollably and feeling

I needed to run away. Holy Name Academy was beside Tampa Bay. All I needed to get back to Cuba was a small boat.

My parents never witnessed my first date, my first formal gown. When I was sick, I was alone. Later, I realized that this was the only way for them to provide me with an excellent education. Throughout those crucial years from childhood to adulthood, I kept thinking about Cuba and the home I had left behind. Cuba matters to me!

3

Latin American Journey:
from Redneck to Yuma

JAY S. BRICKMAN

No single great epiphany occurred in developing my thoughts and subsequent work on US-Cuban relations. My opinions about the relations of the United States with Latin America, and specifically with Cuba, reflect my life's experiences. While Maria Conchita was dramatically impacted by the Cuban Revolution, as were many other people with whom we have worked in developing bridges between the United States and Cuba, my initial exposure to revolution came from a very different place, although parallel in time.

If we agree that a revolution is a total or radical change, then my world, the southern United States, was itself undergoing a revolution in the 1960s. A glance at the headlines shows the depth of what was happening:

- Sit-ins across the Southeast, 1960
- Freedom Riders jailed in Mississippi, 1961
- Voter-registration organizing faces resistance from the White Citizens' Council and the Ku Klux Klan, 1962
- The Albany Movement, 1962
- The Birmingham Campaign, 1962–64

- March on Washington, highlighted by Martin Luther King's "I have a dream" speech, 1963
- Governor Wallace tries to block integration at the University of Alabama, and President Kennedy is forced to send troops, 1963
- Mississippi Freedom Summer, 1964
- Civil Rights Act of 1964

This was an internal war for civil rights, taking place in the United States at the same time as the Cuban Revolution. What does it have to do with Cuba? In my case, it provided the awakening to social change. I was studying international economics and Latin American affairs at the University of Florida, where I found an intellectual interest in what was happening in Cuba. While Fidel Castro and Che Guevara were revolutionaries challenging the Cuban establishment, people like Martin Luther King Jr., Malcolm X, Rosa Parks, Robert Kennedy, and President John F. Kennedy were saying we all needed to think about what it means to be a citizen in your own country.

Coming from the Deep South and studying at a university that was just then moving toward integration, I found that the theme of integration was not an intellectual curiosity, but rather a visceral experience. It meant that I really had to look inside myself and think about human relations and change. Dr. Alfred Clubok was my senior honors sponsor at the University of Florida, and we had long discussions about what was happening in the country. Out of these discussions came the idea to write my senior thesis about a city that was not burning: my hometown of Mobile, Alabama.

Despite what was happening in Selma, Montgomery, and Birmingham—escalating tensions and official mishandling of peaceful protests—Mobile, for some reason, was very different. We set up a plan for me to go home and try to understand the dynamics taking place in racial relations and social change in Mobile. In many ways, what was happening in the South was similar to what was going on in Cuba; economic development was divided very much along racial lines. While a relatively small group benefited from the system, a large segment of the population was basically disenfranchised.

In my fieldwork, I saw how strong the feelings were on both sides, and I learned some basic ideas about conflict resolution. First, if you want to understand a person, a movement, or a country, it is important to understand the history and the culture. Second, "revolutionary" change can take place if individuals are prepared to make the commitment to support change. You need groups of people to make a movement, but individuals have to provide the spark and cultivate the environment for change. Third, there are several roads to revolution, and those roads can be relatively peaceful or violent.

Thus many of my views were formed as a result of a senior thesis done in April 1964. As a side note, because that experience taught me how important education can be, I have supported Harvard's David Rockefeller School of Cuban Studies. I also supported Cuban studies at the University of Florida. Cuban issues, which are studied at the university, have been an interesting facet of Florida politics.

Perspectives gained via that senior thesis helped prepare me for the next step in my development in relation to Latin America. After graduation from Florida, I was awarded a fellowship to attend Johns Hopkins for graduate school. I didn't want to just read about Latin America, but to be there, and it started on a Greyhound bus.

My parents were recovering from a difficult economic period. They had lost their business, so the question was how much money did I have? With some savings from my time in the army, plus money from part-time jobs in Gainesville, I was determined that I could take a Greyhound bus to Laredo, walk across the border, and find a bus to Mexico City. Buses in Mexico today are a comfortable way to travel, with air-conditioning, bathrooms, movies, reclining seats, and even attendants. In 1964, you survived the bus by piling in and holding on.

From Laredo to Mexico City was a two-lane highway, stops all along the way, no air-conditioning, and almost twenty hours to go 698 miles. Yes, there were chickens on board. I got my first taste of freshly fried *chicharrones* (pork cracklings) from a roadside vendor. My seat companion, a Mexican housewife, gave me a long lecture on why Mexican wives expected their husbands to hit them. This was my first exposure to the three *F*s: *feo, fuerte, y fiel* (ugly, strong, and loyal).

Hungry, I arrived at the bus station on Insurgentes and La Reforma in Mexico City. As I got off the bus, a small boy approached and asked, "Que hora es?" Ten minutes later, it occurred to me that he had asked what time it was. From that confidence-building moment, I found a taxi to take me to Antonio Sola number 41 in Colonia Condesa. *La señora* Vidal greeted me with one simple question: did I really want to learn Spanish? Yes, I told her.

"Bueno," she said. "*Entonces eso es la última vez que hablamos en inglés.*" *That's the last time we speak English.* Right. That told me what time it was. The Mexico experience could not have been better.

The Vidals not only insisted that I really learn Spanish (what patience!) but also took me to every social event with the family. Weddings, baptisms, wakes, birthday parties—wherever they went, Jay was sure to follow. Because of my proclivity for using catsup on all food, I became known as "catsup Jay," which was, at least, a little better than *gringito*.

The Mexico experience was formative in so many ways. The Spanish was invaluable, but perhaps even more important was that for the first time, I was able to see the United States with other eyes. I took classes at the Universidad de Las Americas located near Toluca during that time period. The school had a really diverse student body. We spent long hours out of class talking about social movements and debating issues such as Coca-Cola and *Chispa de la Muerte* (the spark of death) giving rise to labor action and consumer boycotts. Needless to say, Fidel Castro was a central figure in many of these discussions in the mid-1960s.

I would take all these issues to my Mexican home and get yet another point of view from the Vidals. They were originally from Catalonia in Spain, and they had strong opinions on everything. None of these discussions made me love my country less, but they did show me that other people had different views about US policies and culture.

All too soon it was time to board another Greyhound and make my way to Washington to begin graduate school. Those bus rides have since served as my underlying reason to work hard—so that I could fly (although today, bus upgrades and air travel complications suggest that the bus may be the better alternative). I went to the School of Advanced International Studies at Johns Hopkins, and my stay there simply underlined for me the importance of education, both in and out of the classroom.

So much was going on in Washington during the 1960s: the Cold War, the Vietnam War, the Civil-Rights movement, and the question about who "gave away Cuba?" In this period, two things very much impressed me regarding Cuba specifically and foreign policy in general. The first realization came from talking with one of my classmates, Tuna Kathleen Wieland, whose father was William A. Wieland, the man accused of aiding Fidel Castro's rise to power. I have no idea about what Mr. Wieland did or did not do, but I certainly saw the impact on his daughter. It made me wonder about how one person could be so influential as to give Cuba away, and it also made me think about whether Cuba was "ours" to give away.

The second realization came from Senator J. William Fulbright, who had an informal chat with us on foreign policy. One of the topics was Vietnam and why he no longer supported the Gulf of Tonkin resolution.[1] The senator said he had voted for the resolution because he received a early-morning call from the president advising him that the North Vietnamese had attacked a US vessel, but later, he was not sure that information was correct. In addition, he said he had not visualized how broadly the resolution would be used.

At this time, Senator Fulbright published his book *The Arrogance of Power*, and one of the points he made was, "Throughout our history, two strands have coexisted uneasily, a dominant strand of democratic humanism and a lesser but durable strand of intolerant Puritanism. There has been a tendency throughout the years for reason and moderation to prevail as long as things are going tolerably well or as long as our problems seem clear and finite and manageable. But…when some event or leader of opinion has aroused the people to a state of high emotion, our puritan spirit has tended to break through, leading us to look at the world through the distorting prism of a harsh and angry moralism."[2]

Seldom does one have the opportunity of meeting a truly gifted person. Sen Fulbright was truly gifted. In sharing his experiences he was very clear that it was not unpatriotic to question your governments decisions. In fact, it may be the most patriotic thing you can do. As I have noted, there was not one "aha moment" that made me question the US policy toward Cuba. It was a long process of thought and analysis.

After graduating from Johns Hopkins and a short stay with Cummins Engine Company, I began to work with Chrysler International. The first stop was the Chrysler Institute. My graduation assignment was to be part of the team on a truck convoy called *El Mundo de Camiones* Chrysler. We took our road show about Chrysler from Detroit to Panama City, Panama. Three months on the road—a great way to learn about Central America. From there I was assigned to Mexico City to do price-and-product analysis for Latin America.

Two years later I moved to Managua, Nicaragua, with Quaker Oats, in charge of new-product development for Central America. Living in Managua was again an incredible education. In addition to meeting wonderful people, two incidents greatly affected me: first, the earthquake in Managua on December 22, 1972, and second, the impact of the Sandinista movement. The experience in the earthquake taught me much about how fragile life can be, and it prepared me to devote as much energy as possible to the execution of Operation Rapid Response to aid Port-au-Prince, Haiti, after the earthquake in 2010. The Sandinista movement took me back to my honors thesis.[3] It seemed so obvious that one small group could not enjoy the great majority of the wealth while others lived in abject poverty—a discussion that I continued to have when I moved to Venezuela.

In 1975, I began my career as an entrepreneur at Crowley Maritime. An entrepreneur is a person who never moves into the core business but looks for new opportunities for the company, develops them, and if successful, turns those operations over to core-business managers. This path led me to open and manage services to the Dominican Republic, the US Virgin Islands, the eastern Caribbean, Haiti, Venezuela, Colombia, Mexico, and Cuba. Tom Crowley Sr. had an interest in Cuba. He had purchased a ship that had been in the Cuban trade, and when he purchased Trailer Marine Transport, he set up a shipping network in the Caribbean and asked me to look into Cuba. That was the trailhead on my path to being nicknamed a *yuma*.

In 1975, Kirby Jones obtained State Department permission to take a business group to Cuba.[4] I joined the trip and came away with a stronger feeling than ever that US policy was not good for the United States. From a business point of view, there was not much we could do, but I continued to work on how Crowley could approach a business relationship with Cuba and how else I might influence a change in policy.

In the meantime, I had moved from Jacksonville to Puerto Rico to Venezuela to New York to Jacksonville to New Orleans to Miami to Jacksonville and finally back to Mexico, where I managed the operations in Mexico, Colombia, and Venezuela. During this time, it became obvious that changes were occurring in US relations with Cuba, and my focus on Cuba sharpened.

4

Cuba Matters

On December 17, 2014, the White House Fact Sheet reflected a new course for the relations between Cuba and the United States. Then on April 14, 2015, the White House announced that President Barack Obama had officially recommended removal of Cuba from the list of state sponsors of terrorism, initiating the essential first steps for normalization of relations after more than fifty-five years of hostilities. However, it is only the first step. Many challenges still lie ahead. These difficult tasks will require some of the key concepts in dealing with Cuba—passion, persistence, and patience (see chapter eight). Why should both countries devote so much effort to normalizing relations? Simply stated, because both have much to gain.

A rare poll of Cubans living on the island was conducted by Bendixen & Amandi, which came out April 2015 on behalf of the networks Univision and Fusion. They wanted to know the views of the reforms announced by President Obama in December 2014. A near unanimous 97 percent of those interviewed said that better relations with the United States would benefit the Cuban people. Nearly the same percentage agreed that the economic embargo should be lifted. According to the study, 73 percent of Cubans feel optimistic about the future, and 70 percent would like to start their own businesses, with 37 percent hoping to do so in the next five years.

Changes in policy open up avenues in both directions for investment and trade, thus benefiting both countries. We can venture to say that stable economies create stable neighbors. The close proximity of the two countries makes each an attractive market for the other. At 11.5 million people, Cuba has the largest Caribbean population, providing the United States a new export market. The United States represents a population of over three hundred million for Cuban exports.

And beyond trade and investment, why else does it matter?

It matters in the international arena: In October 2014, in the United Nations 193-nation assembly, 188 countries voted for the nonbinding resolution titled "Necessity of Ending the Economic, Commercial, and Financial Embargo Imposed by the United States of America against Cuba." This might be a vote against the United States or in favor of Cuba, but in either case, it illustrates how the US policy of isolation is isolating the United States.

Speaking at the UN in 2013 on behalf of the European Union, Rita Kazragiené of Lithuania said US legislation had "extended the effects of the embargo to third countries. The European Union continuously opposed such extraterritorial measures. While appreciating small measures that lifted remittance obstacles, she could not accept unilaterally imposed restrictions that impeded the European Union's economic and commercial relations with Cuba. Dialogue between Cuba and the European Union had addressed issues, including human rights."[1]

After December 17, 2014, Cuba and the United States have started to move away from this position and have begun unraveling the policy of the last fifty years. This growing cooperation permits both countries to move away from an adversarial relationship at the United Nations, taking away the significant irritant of the concept of extraterritoriality by the United States with its European partners.

It matters in the Western hemisphere: President Barack Obama called on Congress on December 17, 2014, to consider lifting the economic embargo that has been in place for more than five decades. This act by the president is a crucial step toward removing a major obstacle imposed by the United States on its neighbors, Mexico and Canada, which both have strong diplomatic relations with Cuba.

The Summit of the Americas in Cartagena, Colombia, held in April of 2012, was one of a continuing series of summits bringing together the leaders of the Americas, including North America, Central America, the Caribbean, and South America—but not Cuba. In response to the potential controversy sparked by boycotts over the exclusion of Cuba, the hosting Colombian president at the time, President Juan Manuel Santos, flew to Havana, where he got assurances from Raúl Castro that the country would not insist on attendance, which could have embarrassed Colombia.

The Latin American countries mentioned firmly and unanimously that their chairs would be empty at the Seventh Summit of the Americas that was held in Panama in April 2015 if Cuba was not included. President Obama implemented the approval of Cuba's attendance in his December 2014 policy initiative. In chapter ten, we discuss compelling reasons for this initiative, and the continued pressure of the Latin American nations was definitely a factor in its making.

Jorge Montaño of Mexico told the UN in 2013 that his country had "for more than two decades used the assembly to express its opposition to the United States blockade, which was not supported by law. He noted that Cuba had set out plans for the achievement of the Millennium Development Goals despite those sanctions. Stressing his delegation's opposition to the economic blockade of any state, he said that what was happening in Cuba contradicted the ideas and views of his country. Any type of sanctions imposed on any state could only be done by the Security Council."[2]

Our policy of isolating Cuba has long been a defining fixture of Latin American politics, and it has united governments across the hemisphere, regardless of their ideologies. Even some of Washington's close allies in the Americas have rallied to Cuba's side.

For years we have watched Latin American support for the United States slip away. President Obama has suddenly turned the tables by declaring a sweeping détente with Cuba, opening the way for a major repositioning of the United States in the region. Latin American leaders are now describing the president of the United States in new ways. Here is what they had to say, as quoted in the article, "Latin American Leaders Cheer Historic Opening of US-Cuba Relations."

Colombia: Conservative President Juan Manuel Santos applauded both the US and Cuban governments' "courage" through Twitter. "We celebrate the courage and audacity of President Barack Obama and the Cuban government to create a peaceful future in the American continent."

Peru: Left-leaning President Ollanta Humala also celebrated the event. "It's a brave, historic decision that opens a new stage in the process of America's integration."

Mexico: President Enrique Peña Nieto's government released another positive statement, saying the move was a step forward for both countries. "The government of Enrique Peña Nieto celebrates the measures announced by both countries in reference to political dialogue and openness in various aspects."

Argentina: President Cristina Fernández praised the Cuban people for their "courage." Fernández, who just handed over the temporary presidency of Mercosur to Dilma Rousseff, specifically congratulated the Cuban government and its people on behalf of Mercosur (which stands for Southern Common Market, in Spanish). The subregional bloc counts Argentina, Brazil, Paraguay, Uruguay, and Venezuela among its members. She said the process of normalizing relations with the US had been undertaken with "absolute dignity and on an equal standing," according to EFE.

Brazil: President Dilma Rousseff congratulated both countries on the opening of relations. Rousseff heaped praise on both Obama and Castro for the reconciliation. She also gave a shout out to Pope Francis, saying the agreement "sets an example that it is possible to reestablish broken relations."[3]

Cuba matters because Latin Americans have long viewed the US relationship with Cuba as an old vendetta. The United States has not had such favorable acceptance of its hemispheric policy since President John F. Kennedy initiated the Alliance for Progress in 1961.

It matters in US domestic politics: President Obama's move to normalize US-Cuban relations has the potential to reshape presidential politics in the battleground state of Florida by giving Democrats a chance to cultivate new ties with Cuban Americans and to dwell on domestic necessities and not foreign policy.

Guillermo Grenier, a professor at Florida International University who has polled Miami's Cubans since the early 1990s, says the policy change gives Democrats a chance to woo voters who have not been represented in mainstream politics and who want to see normalization.

The Sunshine State will likely play a pivotal role in the 2016 presidential election, and its southern reaches are a heartland of Cuban Americans, who, for decades, threw their weight as a bloc behind anticommunist Republicans.

Finally Obama's action will hopefully bring to an end the political debate regarding US Cuban policy. At the same time, Cuba's domestic policy will be impacted. As President Raúl Castro has noted, with normalization of relations and the eventual revoking of the embargo, the Cuban government will no longer have US policy as an excuse for lack of economic growth in Cuba.

It matters in US-Cuba economic and trade relations: President Obama has not been able to eliminate the embargo, which is enshrined in the Helms-Burton Act. Eliminating the embargo will take an act of the US Congress, but it will happen. It will be a long and tedious process. Many Americans have supported engagement for years, and now President Obama has opened the floodgate! There will be challenges for both sides. The Cubans have implemented new investment guidelines; they have developed the Port of Mariel and are establishing an industrial-development zone. All this enhances investment potential and positions Cuba to have much more to offer than just rum and tobacco. Patience is necessary, and confidence must be built.

US and Cuban biomedical industries could start joint ventures, particularly in cancer research. The steel and aluminum companies in the United States will have immediate access to Cuban nickel. As noted earlier, Cuba gains entry into the US market and represents a new export market of 11.5 million for the United States, especially Florida and the Gulf states. Both countries must recognize that two very different economic and political models remain, and the next challenge is finding ways to work in a complementary manner.

Working together has already become the norm in disaster-response situations, as we discuss in chapter ten. Some may find it ironic that the United States and Cuba have similar philosophies about assisting countries facing catastrophic events who are in need of humanitarian action. For our purposes, the objective now is for Cuba and the United States to act for common interests, not just occasionally in response to disasters but instead as a routine procedure. By developing beneficial political, economic, and social policies, Cuba and the United States can set the stage for improved relations throughout the Americas.

5

New Dynamics

Well before the US policy change announcement on December 17, Cuba acknowledged that its economic model was not viable and began taking significant steps to modernize and liberalize its economic structure within the existing political framework.

Three years ahead of Mr. Obama's announcement, President Raúl Castro commenced economic reforms involving private property ownership. In November 2011, for the first time since the early days of the revolution, Cubans were allowed to buy and sell real estate. Transactions of various kinds, including sales, trades, and gifts to relatives by Cubans who are emigrating, are no longer subject to government approval. Provisions of the new law include the following:

- Instead of going through local housing officials, the buyer and seller complete the necessary real-estate sales agreement before a lawyer. Payment is made through a bank.
- There is a tax associated with the sale. Sellers pay a 4 percent personal income tax on the sale price, and buyers pay a 4 percent property-transfer tax.
- Residents are allowed to own only one residence and a second home in a vacation area.
- People trading homes can pay for the difference in value.

- Cubans who emigrate can transfer or sell homes before leaving the country.
- Transfers and donations in divorce settlements and inheritance have also been revised.

In January 2013, Raúl Castro implemented new Cuban migration rules allowing Cubans to spend more time overseas without forfeiting their Cuban residency, a concession that reflects the government's desire for closer ties with millions of Cubans who live abroad. The new rules eliminate expensive, time-consuming paperwork for most Cubans, who now need only a passport to travel. The Cuban government has allowed some medical professionals to go abroad, though it continues to limit travel by people who work for strategic sectors. Cubans who leave the island will no longer lose their property, and those who wish to return for good can reapply for residency. The government has extended the period that Cubans may spend overseas without losing their right to return to two years, giving them more time to find jobs overseas and creating a window for those in the United States to apply for residency in Cuba.

In anticipation of improved relations with the United States, Cuba has also made some significant infrastructural and legal changes. Working with Brazilian financing, the Cuban government has invested almost a billion dollars to construct a state-of-the-art maritime port and a contiguous industrial-development zone. To encourage foreign direct investment, Cuba has revamped its tax and labor laws. At the same time, it has launched an ambitious project to convert the port of Havana into a world-class cruise port to accommodate the anticipated flow of tourists from the United States.

It is important to both recognize this crescendo of actions in Cuba and to congratulate President Obama on the wise decision to turn over a new leaf in US-Cuba relations. Because of the steps each country has taken, both are poised for further movement, making this is a key time to assess their respective positions and the environment in which the two presidents are working. Mutual respect is imperative, and understanding the history and politics of the relationship between the two countries matters.

The following material is a brief assessment, after which we present key provisions from the White House Fact Sheet, "Charting a New Course on Cuba," and then we discuss the pertinent history (chapter six) and politics (chapter seven).

Jay and Maria: Former congressman Lincoln Díaz-Balart said in an April 2013 interview by the *Miami Herald* that "he did not have confidence that the President of the United States would insist that a genuine democratic transition for the Cuban people would manifest itself before lifting the embargo."[1] On March 6, 1996, the US Congress passed the Helms-Burton Act by 336 to 86 votes, thus curtailing presidential power on foreign policy in regard to Cuba (see chapter seven).

The White House Fact Sheet provides interesting dilemmas. The administration must find common ground in working constructively with the US House and Senate. It must also refrain from mandating changes in the Cuban government.

Since the 1980s, the Cuban policy of the United States has historically been controlled by the Cuban Americans in Congress. With both houses under Republican control in 2015, this clearly becomes a tough battle for the president. We must take into consideration the role that Cuban American congressional representatives and senators play in shaping our policy. President Obama's intentions are admirable, but unfortunately, Miami Mania remains (see chapter seven). The State Department recommended removing Cuba from the terrorist list, and President Obama did so, clearly removing a major obstacle.

Responding to the announcement, President Raúl Castro said, "We have also agreed to renew diplomatic relations. This in no way means that the heart of the matter has been solved. The economic, commercial, and financial blockade, which causes enormous human and economic damages to our country, must cease. Though the blockade has been codified into law, the President of the United States has the executive authority to modify its implementation."[3]

There are several battles to be fought. In order to open an embassy in Havana, the State Department will need the appropriation of funds, which come from a House subcommittee. Kay Granger (R-Texas) chairs the State and Foreign Operations Appropriations Subcommittee in the House, and is involved in other related programs. She has openly criticized the administration decision to act unilaterally. Interestingly, Representative Mario Díaz-Balart, a Cuban American, presently serves on the House Committee on Appropriations and three of its subcommittees, one being the same subcommittee where Representative Kay Granger is chair.

President Obama wants to appoint an ambassador to Cuba. To do that, he has to have the approval of the Senate Foreign Relations Committee. Senator Marco Rubio (R-Florida), a Cuban American descendant, is an important member of the committee. He has promised to derail the White House efforts, and he is a potential GOP presidential candidate. In his response to the White House Fact Sheet, Senator Rubio said, "I anticipate we're going to have a very interesting couple of years discussing how you're going to get an ambassador nominated and how you're going to get an embassy funded."[4]

Representative Ileana Ros-Lehtinen has served on the House Rules Committee since 2013. This committee is one of the oldest and most influential in the House. Unlike traditional committee positions, the majority of its members are directly selected by the speaker of the House, while the minority members are selected by the minority leader. The committee is commonly known as "the speaker's committee" because it is the mechanism the speaker uses to maintain control of the House floor. Its members define the unique procedure governing the consideration of various bills that reach the House floor. Speaker of the House John Boehner said, "Relations with the Castro regime should not be revisited, let alone normalized, until the Cuban people enjoy freedom—and not one second sooner."[6]

As was pointed out by President Raúl Castro, the blockade has been codified into law. President Obama has to obtain the cooperation of Congress to repeal laws concerning the boycott. How much authority he has to modify provisions of the Cuban embargo by altering the Export Administration Regulations (EAR) and the Cuban Assets Control Regulations (CACR) are further questions that arise.

The main dilemma that both Cuba and the United States face is that they must learn to coexist with their differences. Throughout the negotiations, a key element will be mutual respect, something not much in evidence in the past. There has to be an understanding of political realities. For example, on the US side, how much can President Obama really deliver? And on the Cuban side, how much change in domestic policy is the government willing or able to implement? Movement has occurred on both sides, but negotiating the next steps will take staying power. Keep in mind that the United States is not the only country negotiating with Cuba. Christian Leffler, Chief European Negotiator at the European Union–Cuba talks advises that it is really important to "have a clear vision, steady nerves, and tons of patience." Meanwhile, let us consider some of what President Obama actually said.[7]

Fact Sheet: Charting a New Course on Cuba
Establishing diplomatic relations with Cuba

The President has instructed the Secretary of State to immediately initiate discussions with Cuba on the re-establishment of diplomatic relations with Cuba, which were severed in January 1961.

In the coming months, we will re-establish an embassy in Havana and carry out high-level exchanges and visits between our two governments as part of the normalization process. US engagement will be critical when appropriate and will include continued strong support for improved human rights conditions and democratic reforms in Cuba and other measures aimed at fostering improved conditions for the Cuban people.

The United States will work with Cuba on matters of mutual concern and that advance US national interests, such as migration, counter narcotics, environmental protection, and trafficking in persons, among other issues. The US Constitution divides the foreign policy powers between the President and Congress so that both share in the making of foreign policy. The executive and legislative branches each play important roles that are different but that often overlap. Both branches have continuing opportunities to initiate and change foreign policy, and the interaction between them continues indefinitely throughout the life of a policy.

Adjusting regulations to more effectively empower the Cuban people

The changes announced today will soon be implemented via amendments to regulations of the Departments of the Treasury and Commerce. Our new policy changes will further enhance our goal of empowering the Cuban population.

Our travel and remittance policies are helping Cubans by providing alternative sources of information and opportunities for self-employment and private property ownership, and by strengthening independent civil society.

These measures will further increase people-to-people contact; further support civil society in Cuba; and further enhance the free flow of information to, from, and among the Cuban people. Persons must comply with all provisions of the revised regulations; violations of the terms and conditions are enforceable under US law.

Facilitating an expansion of travel under general licenses for the twelve existing categories of travel to Cuba authorized by law

General licenses will be made available for all authorized travelers in the following existing categories: (1) family visits; (2) official business of the US government, foreign governments, and certain intergovernmental organizations; (3) journalistic activity; (4) professional research and professional meetings; (5) educational activities; (6) religious activities; (7) public performances, clinics, workshops, athletic and other competitions, and exhibitions; (8) support for the Cuban people; (9) humanitarian projects; (10) activities of private foundations or research or educational institutes; (11) exportation, importation, or transmission of information or information materials; and (12) certain export transactions that may be considered for authorization under existing regulations and guidelines.

Travelers in the twelve categories of travel to Cuba authorized by law will be able to make arrangements through any service provider that complies with the US Treasury's Office of Foreign Assets Control (OFAC) regulations governing travel services to Cuba, and general licenses will authorize provision of such services.

The policy changes make it easier for Americans to provide business training for private Cuban businesses and small farmers and provide other support for the growth of Cuba's nascent private sector. Additional options for promoting the growth of entrepreneurship and the private sector in Cuba will be explored.

Facilitating remittances to Cuba by US persons

Remittance levels will be raised from $500 to $2,000 per quarter for general donative remittances to Cuban nationals (except to certain officials of the government or the Communist party); and donative remittances for humanitarian projects, support for the Cuban people, and support for the development of private businesses in Cuba will no longer require a specific license.

Remittance forwarders will no longer require a specific license.

Authorizing expanded commercial sales/exports from the United States of certain goods and services

The expansion will seek to empower the nascent Cuban private sector. Items that will be authorized for export include certain building materials for private residential construction, goods for use by private-sector Cuban entrepreneurs, and agricultural equipment for small farmers. This change will make it easier for Cuban citizens to have access to certain lower-priced goods to improve their living standards and gain greater economic independence from the state.

Authorizing American citizens to import additional goods from Cuba

Licensed US travelers to Cuba will be authorized to import $400 worth of goods from Cuba, of which no more than $100 can consist of tobacco products and alcohol combined.

Facilitating authorized transactions between the United States and Cuba

US institutions will be permitted to open correspondent accounts at Cuban financial institutions to facilitate the processing of authorized transactions.

The regulatory definition of the statutory term "cash in advance" will be revised to specify that it means "cash before transfer of title;" this will provide more efficient financing of authorized trade with Cuba.

US credit and debit cards will be permitted for use by travelers to Cuba.

These measures will improve the speed, efficiency, and oversight of authorized payments between the United States and Cuba.

Initiating new efforts to increase Cubans' access to communications and their ability to communicate freely

Cuba has an Internet penetration of about 5 percent—one of the lowest rates in the world. The cost of telecommunications in Cuba is exorbitantly high, while the services offered are extremely limited.

The commercial export of certain items that will contribute to the ability of the Cuban people to communicate with people in the United States and the rest of the world will be authorized. This will include the commercial sale of certain consumer communications devices, related software, applications, hardware, and services, and items for the establishment and update of communications-related systems.

Telecommunications providers will be allowed to establish the necessary mechanisms, including infrastructure, in Cuba to provide commercial telecommunications and Internet services, which will improve telecommunications between the United States and Cuba.

Updating the application of Cuba sanctions in third countries

US-owned or -controlled entities in third countries will be generally licensed to provide services to, and engage in financial transactions with, Cuban individuals in third countries. In addition, general licenses will unblock the accounts at US banks of Cuban *nationals who have relocated outside of Cuba; permit US persons to participate in third-country professional meetings and conferences related to Cuba; and allow foreign vessels to enter the United States after engaging in certain humanitarian trade with Cuba, among other measures.*

Pursuing discussions with the Cuban and Mexican governments to discuss our unresolved maritime boundary in the Gulf of Mexico

Previous agreements between the United States and Cuba delimit the maritime space between the two countries within 200 nautical miles from shore. The United States, Cuba, and Mexico have extended continental shelf in an area within the Gulf of Mexico where the three countries have not yet delimited any boundaries.

The United States is prepared to invite the governments of Cuba and Mexico to discuss shared maritime boundaries in the Gulf of Mexico.

Initiating a review of Cuba's designation as a State Sponsor of Terrorism

The President has instructed the Secretary of State to immediately launch such a review, and provide a report to the President within six months regarding Cuba's support for international terrorism. Cuba was placed on the list in 1982. [President Obama removed Cuba from the list on April 14, 2015.]

Addressing Cuba's participation in the 2015 Summit of the Americas in Panama

President Obama participated in the Summit of the Americas in Panama. Human rights and democracy were key Summit themes. Cuban civil society was allowed to participate along with civil society from other countries participating in the Summit, consistent with the region's commitments under the Inter-American Democratic Charter. The United States welcomed a constructive dialogue among Summit governments on the Summit's principles.

President Raúl Castro, while thanking President Obama, mentioned that Cuba won the war! He offered no concessions for improvement of Cuba's human-rights record, nor did he agree to a blanket policy opening the telecommunications industry. What Raúl requested was the return of the Guantanamo Bay Naval Base; unconditional elimination all economic sanctions; economic compensation for the cost of the economic embargo— which Cuba estimates at 166 billion dollars and growing—removal of Cuba from the State Department terrorist-country list, which has now happened; and a repeal of the embargo.

Keep in mind we are talking about two countries.

6

Historical Discord

History matters. Sooner or later, we need to stop replaying the historical relationship between Cuba and the United States; that is, we need to stop holding parallel conversations that never converge except in the form of collision. But to do so, we must understand the history that underlies the relationship, as illustrated by President Obama and President Raúl Castro at the Summit of the Americas in April 2015.

A good place to start is the Monroe Doctrine. This famous underpinning that shaped US policy toward Latin America is full of irony. The doctrine was originally outlined nearly two hundred years ago, on December 2, 1823, by President James Monroe in his seventh annual message to Congress. Although it was destined to become known as the cornerstone of US-Latin American policy, it had its roots elsewhere entirely. It was developed to resolve a conflict between the United Kingdom and the United States concerning the northwest coast of North America, and the negotiations were proposed to the two parties by the Russians. The Old World monarchies exercised their conflicts and rivalries in the New World. The very derivation of the document exemplifies why the United States was in need of a policy about European incursions in the Americas. The policy it articulated came to be a source of deep resentment among Latin American nations as being overtly interventionist and imperialistic.

In part, here is what President Monroe said.

At the proposal of the Russian Imperial Government…instructions have been transmitted to the minister of the United States at St. Petersburg to arrange, by amicable negotiation, the respective rights and interest of the two nations on the northwest coast of this continent…In the discussions to which this interest has given rise and in the arrangements by which they may terminate the occasion has been judged proper of asserting, as a principle in which the rights and interest of the United States are involved, that the American continents, by the free and independent condition which they have assumed and maintain, are henceforth not to be considered as subjects for future colonization by any European powers.[1]

Monroe declared that any such attempts would be regarded as "dangerous to our peace and safety" (see appendix 2 for more complete excerpts).

In the same message, President Monroe moved from the Northwest to Latin America, declaring, "It is impossible that the allied powers should extend their political system to any portion of either continent without endangering our peace and happiness; nor can anyone believe that our southern brethren, if left to themselves, would adopt it of their own accord. It is equally impossible, therefore, that we should behold such interposition in any form with indifference."

Viewing the document with hindsight, irony soon crops up again. "It is still the true policy of the United States to leave the parties to themselves, in the hope that other powers will pursue the same course," said Monroe. He could not know the changes that President Theodore Roosevelt would usher into being.

Though Monroe was effectively staking out US hegemony over the Americas, his approach was basically a passive one. Seventy years later, an "adjustment" or corollary to this policy came. Roosevelt stated that the United States "would intervene as a last resort" to ensure that other nations in the Western Hemisphere fulfilled their obligations to international creditors and did not violate the rights of the United States or invite "foreign aggression to the detriment of the entire body of American nations."[2] We live in a small world; this corollary was implemented because of the economic situation in Venezuela in 1904, just as pressures for policy adjustment toward Cuba today are intensifying partly as a result of upheaval in Venezuela. The "Big Stick" was born.

In the late 1800s, the United States was clearly in an expansionist period. Its foreign policy included the open-door policy for China and could correctly be called imperialistic—easy to criticize and certainly reflected in US dealings with Cuba.

It is worth returning to the 1820s to review the historical trajectory of relations between the two countries. Thomas Jefferson warned that if at any point Spain did not continue to control Cuba, the United States should safeguard its own interests there. In 1824, Secretary of State John Quincy Adams said of Puerto Rico and Cuba, "These islands are natural appendages of the North American continent."[3]

There is no question that the United States was an expansionist nation. It was expanding its control across the continent. That was its Manifest Destiny. To our knowledge, no other islands in the Caribbean were considered attachments to US territory as was Cuba. From the US point of view, Cuba commanded the trade routes to the Gulf of Mexico. The United States was intent upon expanding world trade from its Gulf Coast and was concerned about possible European interference in this trade route.

The value of US exports by 1870 was about $392 million. By 1900, exports had increased to almost $1,394 billion. The United States produced more than it could consume and was generating more capital than it could use domestically. The national attitude was well expressed by Secretary of State Richard Olney in a note to England, "Today the United States is practically sovereign on this contingent, and its fiat is law upon the subjects to which it confines its interposition."[4]

Cuba was a good fit with the US expansion plan. The largest island in the Caribbean, Cuba lay ninety miles off the US mainland and belonged to a declining imperial power, Spain. Slave revolts in Haiti forced the French out and effectively destroyed its sugar industry. Spanish Cuba reacted to the Haiti situation by easing trade restrictions, welcoming French planters, and permitting unlimited importation of slaves. In the 1840s, some Cuban planters favored annexation to the United States, which would integrate Cuba into its major market and would also protect Cuba's ability to continue its slave economy.

The US Civil War dampened the Cuban desire to become part of the United States but did not reduce Cuba's desire to be independent of Spain. With the *Grito de Yara*, Cuba entered into a ten-year war against the Spanish, which lasted until 1878. Three aspects of this prolonged war greatly impacted relations between the United States and Cuba. First, the war was destructive to sugar planters, which created a fertile field of US capital looking for opportunities; second, the long war provoked immense patriotism in Cuba; and third, while a tentative peace was concluded by the Treaty of Zanjon, the long war showed that Cuba did not have sufficient power to win its independence from Spain. The formula of US expansion, declining Spanish power, and Cuban desire for independence almost inevitably led to the Spanish-American War.

The United States and Cuba hold different views about how the island obtained its independence from Spain. From the US point of view, we think about the rallying cry "Remember the *Maine*" after the US warship was sunk in Havana Harbor; about Teddy Roosevelt and the Rough Riders; and about the Treaty of Paris, which ceded Puerto Rico and Guam to the United States, gave the United States the right to purchase the Philippine Islands, and granted Cuba independence.

While Cuban history recognizes the role the United States played in their war for independence, the *Grito de Baire* is essential for understanding the revered guerrilla fighters known as the Mambises, who fought for independence from Spain—a fight in which the role of José Martí was absolutely key.[5] We might note another irony here. The war known as the Spanish-American War was the Spanish-American-Cuban War, but "Cuban" seems to be silent.

Although the Treaty of Paris granted Cuba its independence, Article 16 stated that "any obligations assumed in this treaty by the United States with respect to Cuba" would be limited to the time the United States occupied Cuba. Once the occupation ended, the United States would "advise any government established on the island to assume the same obligations."[6] Many felt that Cuba lost its independence after wining the war. Irony reigns again here: the United States did not allow Cuba to participate in the treaty. The treaty recognized Cuba's sovereignty, yet US general William R. Shafter refused to allow Cuban general Calixto García and his troops to participate in the Spanish surrender.

The United States occupied Cuba for five years after the war. From the beginning, the relationship was based on a simple economic fact: the law of supply and demand. Economically, Cuba was greatly impacted by US commerce. The United States became its primary market for exports, but also an important source of imports into Cuba. From 1919 through 1933, US businesses dominated Cuba. Investments from US companies increased 526 percent between 1913 and 1928. In 1913, Cuba had thirty-nine US-owned sugar mills. While the majority was Cuban owned, they produced a much smaller amount of sugar than did their American counterparts.[7]

Upon leaving Cuba in 1902 after five years of occupation, the United States insisted that the Platt Amendment become part of the Cuban Constitution. The Platt Amendment was approved on May 22, 1903, and contained the following:

- Cuba would not transfer Cuban land to any power other than the United States.
- Cuba would contract no foreign debt without guarantees that the interest could be served from ordinary revenues.
- The United States had the right of intervention in Cuban affairs and military occupation when US authorities considered that the life, properties, and rights of US citizens were in danger.
- Cuba was prohibited from negotiating treaties with any country other than the United States that would "impair the independence of Cuba."

- Cuba was prohibited from permitting "any foreign power or powers to obtain…judgment in or control over any portion" of Cuba, and the Isle of Pines (now called Isla de la Juventud) was deemed outside the boundaries of Cuba until the title to it was adjusted in a future treaty.
- Lands "necessary for coaling or naval stations at certain specified points to be agreed upon" were to be sold or leased to the United States; the amendment ceded to the United States the naval base at Guantanamo Bay and granted the right to use a number of other naval bases as coal stations.[8]

The Mambises strongly opposed this suite of requirements. They had fought for an independent Cuba, sovereign and in control of its own destiny.

Most clauses of the Platt Amendment were eventually repealed with the 1930s advent of a "good neighbor" policy. But until then, before any presidential election in Cuba, the United States vetted the candidates. Secretary of War Elihu Root characterized the Cubans as a "mass of ignorant and incompetent people," and US policy was designed to promote conservative control of Cuba by US-designated Cubans.[9]

The political and economic climate that existed from 1898 to 1959 based on agreements implemented by the United States on Cuba evolved into the complicated relationship that exists today. It proved a collision path. Given Cuba's proximity to the United States, its harbors were of strategic importance, and the United States wanted to ensure that European powers did not intervene in the Americas. The greatest irony of all that the very policy that was designed to keep foreign powers out of Cuba would foster the entry of the Soviet Union and usher in the Cuban Missile Crisis.

After the Spanish-American War, US annexation was a vision shared by some Cubans, who believed it would bring stability and wealth. The US government would not allow US interests in Cuba to suffer, and these Cubans felt that peace in Cuba could come only through intervention. The

US's train of thought was that turning Cuba over to the Cuban population went against the better judgment of the Cuban upper classes.[10]

The point of this abbreviated history is that, at some level, the US's stance was that we "kind of" owned Cuba, and the Cubans should have listened to us. From the Cuban point of view, of course, Cubans did not belong to anyone.

These factors drove the situation well before Fidel Castro and his 26th of July Movement, and his actions were certainly not just about relations between the United States and Cuba. It was about corruption, government incompetence, and economic inequality, as well as the enormous US influence in Cuba.

After the 26th of July Movement gained momentum, events moved fast, as indicated in the following short anatomy of the run-up to the trade embargo:

- March 1958—The United States prevents sales of arms to the Batista government.
- January 1, 1959—Batista flees Cuba.
- January 7, 1959—United States recognizes the new revolutionary government.
- April 15–26, 1959—Fidel Castro visits the United States and meets with Vice President Richard Nixon for three and a half hours; President Dwight Eisenhower refuses to meet with Fidel Castro.
- May 17, 1959—The first agrarian reform law delivers large-scale expropriation of mostly American-owned land; compensation is offered by the Cuban government but is rejected by the US companies.
- September 4, 1959—US Ambassador Bonsal meets with Fidel Castro to express concern about treatment of US businesses.
- July 1960—The United States reduces the sugar quota by seven hundred thousand tons, apparently to punish Cuba; the Soviet Union agrees to purchase Cuba's sugar; foreign-owned refineries in Cuba refuse to process Soviet oil.

- July 1–17, 1960—US oil refineries, sugar refineries, and banks in Cuba are nationalized.
- October 1960—The United States imposes an embargo covering all commodities except medical supplies and certain food products; in turn, on October 25, Cuba nationalizes all remaining US businesses without compensation.
- January 3, 1961—The United States responds to the arrest and expulsion of two diplomats and withdraws diplomatic relations by closing its embassy in Havana.
- February 7, 1962—The Kennedy Administration strengthens the embargo by adding additional constraints.[11]

Why did the United States break diplomatic relations with Cuba but not with other countries that took similar steps in nationalizing US companies, imposing agrarian reforms, and taking control of their natural resources? As an example, in 1938, the Mexican government expropriated foreign control oil resources in Mexico, with minimal compensation in 1942.

Several other interesting questions arise. At the time of the Cuban Revolution, the US government and the United Fruit Company had recently overthrown the Arbenz government in Guatemala (1954). Did officials think they could do the same in Cuba? How might it have changed the outworking if Eisenhower had received Fidel on his first trip to the United States? Or if Nixon had not confronted Fidel? Or if it had been understood that nationalism and socialism were not communism?

Instead, the historical paths led to the standoff between the US's "You listen to us" and Castro's "No," which soon devolved into Cuban dependence on the Soviet Union and the United States imposing its trade embargo. Had the United States embargo not been in place, would the political climate in Latin America be different?

Moving up to the recent past, on January 24, 2013, Russian President Vladimir Putin emphasized Cuba's growing role in Latin American regional affairs and welcomed the country's presidency of the Community of Latin American and Caribbean States for the year in the person of President Raúl Castro Ruz.

David versus Goliath is how most of the rest of the world views Cuba, the tiny island in the Caribbean that stood up to the mighty United States. In November 2013, US Secretary of State John Kerry declared the era of the Monroe Doctrine "over," clearly implying a new era in US-Cuban relations. In December 2014, President Barack Obama reaffirmed his commitment in a new US-Cuba policy. The Republican Congress will either embrace or reject the president's initiative, depending on the actions of Cuban American congressional delegation members who hold key committee positions. Most of those committee members belong to Miami Mania, to which we now turn.

7

Miami Mania

Miami, we submit that without Fidel Castro, there would have been no Miami Mania, defined as the very focused and sometimes fanatical effort to remove Fidel and Raúl Castro from the Cuban government structure. Is he a communist? Was he a communist? He is the one qualified to answer that, but this we know: the force of Fidel Castro's ideas and actions drove 135,000 Cuban citizens to Miami between January 1959 and April 1961. This first wave of mass migration became the core of Miami Mania.

Many in this first wave did not expect to stay in Miami for long—perhaps a year, perhaps two. There were two great surprises in store for this group and for the US government too. First, they did not seem to understand Fidel Castro's radical political and economic views. Second, they never suspected he would maintain power for more than fifty years.

In their fervor to overturn the Castro regime, many first-generation Cuban Americans in South Florida tended to overlook the fact that the Batista regime had done away with freedom of the press, had suspended all constitutional rights, and had operated the notorious firing squads that killed and tortured thousands of civilians in the late 1950s, as described in the magazine *Bohemia*. Rafael Díaz-Balart, the father of former congressman Lincoln and current congressman Mario Díaz-Balart, served as undersecretary of interior during Batista's regime. Their aunt, Mirta Díaz-Balart, was married to Fidel Castro. It is suspected that Batista fled to the Dominican Republic with around three hundred million dollars.

It is well worth reading Castro's *History Will Absolve Me* speech, given in a Cuban court in 1953, to better understand his political and economic views (see appendix 1 for excerpts). On capitalism, he said, "The capitalists insist that the workers remain under the yoke."

On the people, he said, "When we speak of the people, we are not talking about those who live in comfort, the conservative elements of the nation. Those ministers can chat away in a Quinta Avenida mansion until not even the dust of the bones of those whose problems require immediate solution remains."[1]

On foreign investment, Castro said, "More than half of our most productive land is in the hands of foreigners. In Oriente, the largest province, the lands of the United Fruit Company and the West Indian Company link the northern and southern coasts. There are two hundred thousand peasant families who do not have a single acre of land to till to provide for their starving children."

On centralized government, he said, "A revolutionary government backed by the people...would proceed immediately to the country's industrialization."

THE FLOW OF CUBANS TO SOUTH FLORIDA

While Fidel Castro's Cuba had a revolution, it planted the seeds of a counterrevolution in Miami. The radicalization of the Cuban Revolution provoked a huge exodus from Cuba to the United States. After the first wave of 135,000 Cubans arrived in the United States between 1959 and 1961, further immigrant arrivals swelled the number to 340,000 by 1973. About 80 percent of those who immigrated chose Miami and South Florida as their home. Miami was being converted from a resort city to a leading city in Latin America. The next large wave of Cubans came to Miami with the Mariel boatlift in 1980. The boatlift was the catalyst that changed the Cuban American community from one looking at how they could change things in Cuba to one that was politically active in taking control of US foreign policy toward Cuba. The 1990s brought another surge of immigrants.

The Cubans who came to the United States in the early 1960s are colloquially known as the Old Guard. Highly educated and white, the first migrants belonged to the upper and middle classes. These Cuban elites completely abandoned their ways of life on the understanding that their exit was merely temporary; they never imagined that the US government would permit Fidel Castro to remain in power. They loved their homeland and were a proud group of exiles, mostly refusing any financial or social assistance from the US government. Religion played an important role in their lives, as did support for one another. With this first wave of exiles, Cuba's professional talent was drained.

Some regard the Cubans who came to the United States during the so-called Freedom Flights of 1965–73 as a separate group, but we have elected to include them with the Old Guard.[2] As this combined first wave of Cuban exiles started to prosper, they took an interest in the political arena, and to this day they control South Florida politics, giving them tremendous influence over US policy toward Cuba. A large number of the Old Guard and their families have never returned to Cuba.

The second great wave brought the Marielitos, those who came during the massive Mariel boatlift in 1980.[3] The surge was precipitated by housing and job shortages. Castro announced on April 20, 1980, that all those who wished to leave Cuba could do so if they had someone willing to pick them up. An estimated 125,000 Cubans arrived on US shores.

Some seventeen hundred boats departed for Cuba as people in the exile community rushed to hire boats in Miami and Key West to pick up their relatives. Multiple boats were overcrowded and barely seaworthy. The massive exodus created negative political fallout for President Jimmy Carter when it was discovered that some of the exiles came from Cuban jails and mental institutions. The boatlift was an overwhelming endeavor; many of the new arrivals had to be placed in refugee camps, and more than seventeen hundred were held in federal prisons as they underwent deportation hearings. Around 590 Marielitos were detained until the government found sponsors for them. The majority of Marielitos were decent, hardworking families who, unfortunately, had to bear the stigma that was synonymous with criminals, prisoners, and the mentally ill.

The background of the Marielitos was very different from that of the Old Guard. Twenty years had gone by under Castro's government. These immigrants had grown up in a socialist society; many were poor and unskilled. They also disappointed the Miami exile community in lacking the spirit of freedom fighters. Not all found Miami to be congenial. Some moved to other cities, and some opted to return to Cuba. While their political influence has increased, they are not part of the Old Guard and are viewed with suspicion by the Cuban establishment. They travel to Cuba to visit their families, and they invest in the small businesses that are now opening up in Cuba.

Cubans in the third and most recent wave entering the United States either enter legally by winning the *bombo* (lottery) or come in under the wet foot/dry foot policy.[4] The latter is a consequence of May 1995 revisions by the Clinton Administration to the Cuban Adjustment Act of 1966 (see appendix 3). Basically Cuban migrants apprehended at sea are returned to Cuba, while those who reach US soil are allowed to stay. These immigrants of the third wave grew up under the Cuban regime, and the Old Guard view them as looking for an easy way out, and as having come for economic and not political reasons. They, too, go to Cuba regularly. They facilitate and finance small-business startups with their relatives back home. They go on vacations to Cuba or serve as mules taking merchandise back.

Maria: It seems that as soon as they set foot on US soil, they turn around and travel back to Cuba, thus creating a tremendous amount of resentment within those who came in the '60s and '70s. They are perceived as *oportunistas* who came to the United States with a different set of values and ethics than those who left Cuba in the 1960s and 1970s.

So with the Marielitos, we had seventeen hundred boats and seventeen hundred criminals—in effect, each embarkation brought one criminal.

So different from the Old Guard of the first wave. I remember how my uncles studied until late in the evenings to pass their medical and bar exams. After a few years of sacrifice, they assimilated into US society, if not its culture. At home we spoke Spanish, but it was seen as important to know a second language.

Our loudness, our gaiety, and those huge family events where everyone talks at the same time are distinctively part of the Cuban culture. Education was a priority as we grew up. Any *B* on our report cards was unacceptable. To my parents, an *A* was the equivalent of a *B+*. Our dad laid down the rule that we had to obtain a college education. It never occurred to us not to attend a university.

Jay: OK, Maria, let's be fair. A lot of prominent individuals arrived in the boatlift. Let me name just a few: Mirta Ojito, who won a Pulitzer Prize; the poet Reynaldo Arenas; and Elizabeth Caballero, the opera singer.

Maria: I agree with your assessment, Jay, but that does not change the connotation associated with the name *Marielitos*. I, for one, have tried to help numerous Cubans who have recently arrived from the island, and when I call other Cubans to help them find employment, the first thing out of their mouths is, "That's another Marielito."

Jay: *Por Dios*, she never lets me have the last word!

Maria: And as for the new arrivals of the 1990s—in order for them to survive in Cuba, they had to steal from the state, or, as most Cubans say, *resolver*.[5] Unfortunately, some of them continued with the same practices after they left Cuba. Some of those who come to the United States today know all the loopholes in the system and feel entitled.

In contrast, I distinctly remember one evening shortly after our arrival, when my dad wrote a check to the US government as repayment for the assistance provided. Many Cubans who arrived during that early period repaid the government, in contrast to what happens today.

CUBAN ADJUSTMENT ACT

While Cuba solidified its relationship with the Soviet Union, Cuban immigration to the United States greatly increased. From 1960 to 1979, hundreds of thousands of Cubans left Cuba for the United States. The Cuban Adjustment Act of 1966 provided more than $1.3 billion of direct financial aid. With the current US-Cuba negotiations, changes or complete abolishment of the act will probably take place.

In a bulletin issued in March 1962, William L. Mitchell, commissioner of Social Security, describes how the Cuban Refugee Program came about. President Eisenhower appointed Tracy S. Voorhees, undersecretary of the army from August 1949 to April 1950, as his personal representative for Cuban refugees. Under his direction, the Cuban Refugee Emergency Center was born. In his final report to the president, he concluded that "the refugee problem had assumed proportions requiring national attention." Under President John F. Kennedy on February 3, 1960, the Cuban Refugee Program was implemented.

At President Kennedy's direction, US Secretary of Health, Education, and Welfare, Abraham A. Ribicoff, was instructed to take the following measures:

- Provide all possible assistance to voluntary relief agencies.
- Obtain the assistance of private and governmental agencies to provide employment opportunities.
- Provide supplemental funds for resettlement.
- Furnish financial assistance to meet basic maintenance requirements of needy Cuban families.
- Provide essential health services.
- Furnish federal assistance for local public-school operating costs.
- Initiate needed measures to augment training and educational opportunities.
- Provide financial aid for the care and protection of unaccompanied children.
- Undertake a surplus food distribution program to be administered by the county welfare authorities.

During the 1960s and 1970s, most Cubans saw any financial assistance as shameful, and if accepted, it was only temporarily.

Maria: Unfortunately that is not the case with most of the Cubans arriving today.

A number of other programs were also set up to aid Cuban refugees. The Cuban communities in South Florida and Union City, New Jersey, took advantage of these programs, while at the same time working to establish both an economic and a political base for the immigrants. Practically all Cuban exiles who have been admitted to the United States have received a special parole, exercised by the attorney general, that grants them full legal status under the law and puts them on a path to citizenship. No other migrant group has enjoyed this privilege.

CUBAN AMERICAN ECONOMIC AND POLITICAL IMPACT

Cubans have transformed Miami from a small laid-back town into an international business center with a considerable Cuban flavor. Members of the growing Cuban population in Miami have remained loyal to their roots, maintaining their norms, culture, religious affiliations, and language. In the process, they transformed Miami into the "Capital of the Americas."

Many of the first-generation Cuban exiles enjoy economic success that has empowered them politically. Cubans represent but a fraction of the growing Hispanic population, yet, at the same time, this first generation of exiles has been extraordinarily successful. The Cuban culture is on display throughout the United States, all the way from Cuban cigars to salsa star Celia Cruz (with her trademark shout of "Azucar!"), the long musical career and international acclaim of Gloria Estefan, and the acting triumphs of Andy Garcia.

Cubans are just as aggressive in the political arena, and the great majority of Cuban American elected officials have expressed strong opposition to travel to Cuba by American tourists and US trade or dialogue with Cuba. The rapid growth of political empowerment in regard to Cuban policy has been phenomenal. In one generation Cuban Americans have been elected to four US Senate seats; five seats in the US House of

Representatives; ten-plus Florida State House seats; three Florida State Senate seats; two Florida Supreme Court judgeships; and as mayors of Miami, Coral Gables, Hialeah, and other communities in Florida. As one observer put it, "Cubans identify with the conquerors, not the conquered; the subject, not the object."[6]

In 1980, Cuban exiles made up more than half the population of Miami, and by the late 1980s, the Cuban American community had become politically dominant in Dade County. Traditionally, from this time onward, it has been a bad idea for any other group to challenge the Cuban community on political issues dealing with the Castro government. Prior to the Cuban influx of the '60s, Mayor Maurice Ferrer, a Democrat of Puerto Rican descent, was Miami's top Hispanic political influence.

The first generation of Cuban American politicians came into an environment that was not politically mature and consisted of one political party, the Democrats. They took over the Republican Party and sponsored candidates for the Florida Legislature. During this period, 68 percent of the Cubans were registered Republicans.[7]

POWER OF THE CUBAN AMERICAN NATIONAL FOUNDATION AND PACS

The Cuban American National Foundation (CANF), led by Jorge Mas Canosa, acted as the only voice of the Cuban exile community. Any other group that wanted to travel to Cuba independently, negotiate with Cuba, trade with Cuba, or establish diplomatic relations was drowned out. Mas Canosa chaired the board of directors from the organization's founding in 1981 until his death in 1997. He was actively engaged with Congress and three administrations, and the involvement ultimately delivered bipartisan support on a firm US-Cuba policy. He was also instrumental in the creation of Radio Marti.

The CANF achieved its first big political coup in 1985, when the Reagan Administration established Radio Marti, named for José Martí, the father of Cuban independence. CANF and its Free Cuba PAC underwrote much of the political process in regard to Cuban policy. The

PAC is a powerful lobbying group that courts both Republicans and Democrats and at the same time donates heavily to their political campaigns. The website www.opensecrets.org shows to whom the PAC has contributed.

Ileana Ros-Lehtinen was the first Cuban American elected to Congress in 1989. Miami was becoming a city with a foreign policy. The Soviet Union was dissolved in late 1991, but by that time, the Cuban American community in South Florida, led by CANF, had become the most dominant voice in determining US policy toward Cuba. Later, the US-Cuban Democracy PAC and other groups became more important in financing political action. In effect, just as the USSR collapsed and the Cold War drew to a close, US policy toward Cuba was captured by the Old Guard, who blamed the Kennedy Administration for the loss at the Bay of Pigs invasion and who labeled the Democratic Party as soft on Castro.

Ileana Ros-Lehtinen, along with others, such as former Senator Bob Menéndez, former representative Lincoln Díaz-Balart, and Representative Mario Díaz-Balart, effectively controlled the legislation related to Cuba. They either prevented bills from coming to the floor for a vote or swayed other congress members and senators to vote against liberalizing relations with Cuba. Their influence has been seen at the executive level as well. This congressional action hinders economic growth for many states. Money talks. Our current policy toward Cuba is shaped to a large degree by political-campaign donations from the Free Cuba PAC.

While CANF has lost much of its original power, the US-Cuba Democracy PAC, formed in 2003, has grown in influence and power. It is a nonpartisan federal political-action committee dedicated to the promotion of an unconditional transition in Cuba to democracy, the rule of law, and the free market. It is one of the largest foreign-policy political committees in the United States and the largest Hispanic political committee in history. The PAC also created the Young Leaders Group on July 30, 2013. Its mission statement is as follows:

The US-Cuba Democracy PAC Young Leaders Group ("YLG") is a group of young professionals and students who work to promote democratic values, human rights, and the rule of law as the cornerstone of US-Cuba policy. The YLG is dedicated to spreading awareness among young Americans regarding the brutality of the Castro dictatorship and the courageous efforts of Cuba's young, vibrant, and diverse prodemocracy movement. Its mission will continue until a free and democratic future is ensured for all Cubans.[8]

Jay: Let's make it clear that there is nothing inappropriate about political PACs. They are not unique, they are not illegal, they are not immoral, and they can serve a very useful purpose. The United States is a country of factions. The import thing to understand is their viewpoints and how they impact foreign policy. James Madison drafted the US Constitution and the Bill of Rights. He was also the father of the Federalist Party and the fourth president of the United States. He wrote, "The latent causes of faction are…sown in the nature of man; and we see them everywhere."[9]

Maria: My concern is that there has not been a counterbalance for a more pragmatic US-Cuba policy. Unless mayority who favor normalized relations unite with the same passion to represent the view of the majority, who basically want the end of the embargo, we will still be mandated by Miami-Mania rules. As a Cuban American, it is disheartening if we do not create a PAC to show our leaders the advantages of changing present policy.

Jay: Let's hope that the negotiations between President Obama and President Raúl Castro will offer the counterbalance that you have suggested is imperative.

MONEY TALKS

Public Campaign, an organization dedicated to reforming campaign financing, published a report in 2009 on how Cuban American money affects Congress. The report claims that candidates who receive money from the Free Cuba PAC "more often than not cast their votes on Cuba policy issues with the hard-liners."

REPORT: HARD-LINE CUBAN AMERICAN MONEY FLOWS TO CONGRESS

The most extensive study of the influence of Cuban American campaign donations finds targeted donations made to members who switched positions and discovers an overall shift of donations to Democrats.

Washington, DC—A report released by Public Campaign today found that a network of hard-line Cuban American individual contributors and a like-minded Political Action Committee (PAC) pumped $10.8 million into federal campaigns since the 2004 election cycle. The report, "Cold Hard Cash, Cold War Politics," is the most extensive look at how the community targets campaign contributions to those in power and to members of Congress who switched their votes toward the hard-liner position.

"In many ways, what we have here is the age-old story of the influence of campaign money in the political process," said David Donnelly, national programs director for Public Campaign, a national nonpartisan watchdog group that advocates for public financing of elections. "This report documents, with indisputable facts, that donations were delivered to a significant number of members of Congress who changed their positions on Cuba policy. Whether we call that a reward, or a campaign donation, it's an indictment of our current pay-to-play system of campaign financing."

The report found that hard-liner Cuban Americans:

- *Gave to at least 337 federal candidates through the US-Cuba Democracy PAC since 2003, 53 percent of whom received reinforcing individual donations from hard-liner Cuban American donors*
- *Vastly increased Cuban Americans' donations to the Democratic Senatorial Campaign Committee (DSCC), and shifted donations to Democrats overall*

- *Targeted donations to recipients whose voting records show a shift in their position on Cuba policy, including seven who took money and switched their positions on dates that were in close proximity to one another*
- *Provided, through the PAC and the network of donors, more than $850,000 to 53 members of Congress who recently publicized their opposition to changes in the policy just weeks before a key committee hearing on travel to Cuba*

"No one should begrudge the ability of all Americans to fully participate in our democracy," said Donnelly. "Yet we should recognize that those with the ability to make large donations have more say over what happens in Washington DC. That is precisely what is happening here. And that is precisely why we need Congress to pass the Fair Elections Now Act."

The bipartisan Fair Elections Now Act (H. R. 1826 and S. 752), introduced by House Democratic Caucus Chair John Larson (D-Connecticut) and Assistant Senate Majority Leader Dick Durbin (D-Illinois), would reduce the fundraising pressures on members of Congress. The bill would allow candidates to voluntarily opt out of the escalating fundraising race and run vigorous campaigns relying on small contributions and limited public funding.[10]

The political power of this group of Cuban Americans is reflected in the Helms-Burton Act. Former congressman Lincoln Díaz-Balart explained in an interview in April 2013 why the embargo is necessary, reaffirming the traditional thinking of the Cuban Old Guard.

At this time, when the democratic opposition within Cuba is acquiring greater strength and showing extraordinary political maturity, I believe it is important to remember the reasons for the existence of the US embargo and the three conditions for its lifting.

When I arrived in the US Congress in January 1993, I was able to confirm that US law did not prohibit trade and financing with the Cuban regime by the great majority of US corporations. I was truly impacted by the fact that US law only prohibited trade and financing with the Cuban regime by foreign subsidiaries of US companies, but not by US companies inside the United States (in other words, the overwhelming majority of US firms).

Mass US tourism to Cuba was also not barred by law. All existing sanctions at that time were contained in executive orders that, of course, could be lifted by other executive orders, at any time, by any president.

Since I was convinced that no dictatorship in history has ever given anything to the democratic opposition in exchange for nothing, and since I did not have confidence that the president of the United States would insist that a genuine democratic transition for the Cuban people be underway before lifting the embargo on the regime, I decided to codify—to enact into law—those executive orders: the prohibitions on commerce, on financing, and on mass US tourism to Cuba. And to condition the lifting of those sanctions (commonly known as the embargo) on three conditions within Cuba: (1) the liberation of all political prisoners, without exceptions; (2) the legalization of all political parties, without exceptions, of the independent press and free labor unions; and (3) the scheduling of free elections with international supervision for the Cuban people.

In March 1996, with the decisive help of Rep. Ileana Ros-Lehtinen and Sen. Bob Menéndez, I achieved codification passed by Congress. All the executive orders that constituted the embargo were made part of US law, as well as the three conditions for their lifting. I believe it was the most important achievement of my eighteen years in the US Congress.

I was convinced then, and I continue to believe, that the US embargo and the conditioning of its lifting—upon the requirement that a genuine democratic transition based on the three conditions be underway in Cuba—constitute instruments of great importance in the hands of the Cuban opposition.[11]

The Obama administration in dealing with Congress has to be knowledgeable of the Helms-Burton Act as well as other laws governing US relations with Cuba. This was underlined in the dialogue between Congresswoman Ileana Ros-Lehtinen and Roberta Jacobson, undersecretary for the Western Hemisphere, when questioned about the Helms-Burton Act.

Jay: Nothing illustrates the Miami Old Guard's position better than the interview with Congressmen Lincoln Díaz-Balart. He wanted to assure that neither his uncle, Fidel Castro, nor Raúl Castro would be in any Cuban government recognized by the United States. Some have characterized this as a family feud that moved across the Florida Straits, but it is a lot more profound than that. It may be a constitutional issue.

Although the Constitution does not explicitly grant presidents the power to recognize foreign governments, it is generally accepted that they have this power as a result of their authority to send and receive ambassadors. Because the acts of sending an ambassador to a country and receiving its representative imply recognition of the legitimacy of the foreign government involved, presidents have successfully claimed exclusive authority to decide which foreign governments will be recognized by the United States. President Obama has taken certain steps to directly challenge Helms-Burton in relations to the embargo, although the ultimate decision resides with Congress.

In addition (and there is some irony here), the much maligned 1902 Platt Amendment, which was repealed in 1934 to ease relations, is back. The Cuban American delegation supported the ability of the United States to decide which prisoners should be released from jail, to determine what political and union structures Cuba should have, and to assure that elections are internationally supervised.

Maria: Now I'm no longer a terrorist, thank you President Obama, since most Cuban Americans had to travel to the island with a Cuban passport issued by the Cuban government.

Jay: To underline the importance of South Florida in state and national policy, in a conversation I had with a former lieutenant governor of Florida, I asked when Tallahassee would support a change in US-Cuba policy. The answer was, "When you people in South Florida change your politics, we in Tallahassee will respond."

SOUTH FLORIDA'S INFLUENCE

The first-generation Cuban exiles in South Florida will tell you that Cuba had a long historical democratic tradition. But examining the historical facts, a different story emerges. From 1492 until 1959, a total of 467 years, there were only twenty-four years in which Cuba qualified as having an elected democratic government.

Yet as the Old Guard continues to dictate much of US policy toward Cuba, the South Florida political spectrum continues to change. The last two presidential elections reflect the change. What will be the outcome of the 2016 presidential election? While the Republican Party won the Cuban American vote, in 2008 and 2012, the Democratic Party carried South Florida. This happened because of the influx of Hispanic immigration from countries other than Cuba; greater participation by the black community; and because the Cuban American community is not a monolithic bloc.

Current US-Cuban policy is clearly articulated by the Old Guard, whose goal is the overthrow of the Castro government. We need to further explore if there is another agenda behind closed doors for some type of normalization. Some organizations have gone as far as drafting government blueprints or proposing elimination of any form of national government in Cuba. Most Cuban American organizations share the same viewpoint—that compromise and dialogue with the current regime are out of the question. Driven by misconceptions of a perfect Cuba prior to Fidel Castro, this is an unnatural political relationship that is in desperate need of a complete overhaul.

Maria: In my opinion, the South Florida politicians and the exiled Cuban Old Guard take the Cuban policy to the absurd. The Miami Cuban

American political influence is an embarrassment for the Florida government. In 2012, the Florida Legislature passed House Bill 959, having been maneuvered into it by the powerful Cuban exile lobby.[12] The bill bars the state of Florida government from hiring foreign firms that do business with Cuba or Syria. However, this being Florida, it was, of course, Cuba in which they had an interest.

As an example of the absurd, Governor Rick Scott, hoping to find favor with the Cuban exile community, ceremoniously signed the measure on May 1, 2012. He then turned around the following week and promptly conceded that the law was unenforceable because only the federal government can pass that kind of international commerce legislation. The bill's cosponsors were Representatives Artiles, J. Diaz, Dorworth, Fresen, Gonzalez, Lopez-Cantera, Nuñez, Oliva, Porth, and Trujillo.

Jay: Parallel to the Florida law, former congressman David Rivera added section 803 to the Defense Appropriations Act of 2013 (HR4310), which would have prohibited US government agencies from entering into contracts with any company that had any dealings with countries on the State Department terrorist list. There was a serious concern that this proposal would be overlooked in the approval of the Defense Appropriations Act of 2013. Had the proposal moved forward, it could have impacted the national defense of the United States directly. What this illustrates is that if there is serious opposition to some of the ideas developed by Cuban American legislators who exemplify Miami Mania, those ideas can be overruled. As we will see in the chapter "Politics and *Pollos*" (chapter nine), if a problem is clearly identified and stakeholders are alerted and united, an alliance to counterbalance Miami Mania can be constructed. Former Congressman Rivera's proposal would have weakened the defense effort of the United States. Once people were alerted to this, there were ample stakeholders who organized successful action to get this wording removed from the Defense Appropriations Act.

It is worth noting how effective Cuban Americans are at protecting their own economic interests as well as at advancing the Old Guard political agenda. "Washington politicians facing a year-end deadline to cut billions in agricultural spending are feuding over the future of food aid for the poor and crop subsidies for farmers," noted reporters in 2013. But they went on. "There is, however, one area of agreement in the contentious negotiations: sugar. Lawmakers decided to preserve the decades-old government safety net that boosts profits for a relatively small group of growers and has cost consumers billions through artificially high prices. The special protection is a testament to the enduring Washington clout of one of the country's wealthiest farming interests, including the politically connected Florida family that controls a substantial share of the world sugar market."[13]

Emotions run high in the Cuban exile community. You only need to visit the Versailles Restaurant or Domino Park in Miami's "Little Havana" to see this. The South Florida community and its politicians are trapped in an emotional limbo. They keep waiting for the death of Fidel and Raúl Castro, as if, by magic, everything in Cuba will change overnight at that point. Today we are witnessing a shift away from the staunch support for Republicans, but key positions within the US Senate and the House are still held by Cuban Americans who completely reject the December 17, 2014, policy changes.

Both President Barack Obama and Raúl Castro are trying to implement more flexible economic and political reforms for the evolution of the current Cuban political system. It behooves the political structure in Miami to show some flexibility at this juncture.

Will the South Florida congressional representatives support funding for a US embassy in Cuba? Will they support the appointment of a US ambassador to Cuba? Will they support the president's action that removes Cuba from the terrorist list? And ultimately, will they permit the repeal of the laws that codify the US embargo on Cuba?

From left my brother Aurelio, Mom (Conchita Alvarez), my brother Tony,
my sister Maggie, Dad (Aurelio Yeyo Piedra), and me.
I must have been six.

The sugar mill in Moron

The chuch in Pina where we attended Mass

My grandparents' home—Pedro Antonio and Tete Alvarez's home

With the Alvarez and Fernandez Morrel side of the family. I'm in the last row, third from the left.

The Piedra Corvison side of the family. I'm sitting on the floor in the first row, first one on the left.

Jay waiting for the first US vessel to enter Cuba after more than forty years

Here comes the Pollos!

Pedro Alvarez Borrego, former chairman and CEO of Alimport, with his staff and Jay (far right)

With the Crowley group, from left to right, Charlie Dominguez, former VP Marketing; Mike Roberts, Legal Council; Alejandro Gonzalez, agent in Cuba; Jorge Estevez, VP Pricing

Crowley containers full of poultry!

My first encounter with Fidel Castro Ruz

At the Havana International Fair; from left: Marcela Jimenez, Gulf South Forest Products, Jay, and me

With a group of children at the fair

People-to-People contact

The famous hand shake between Raúl Castro and President Obama

Jay in the home of the chief of the US Interests Section

*In the home of the chief of the US Interests Section,
by the Maine monument*

Joint rail study with the Cuban Ministry of Transportation:
Pedro Morales, Joseph Threadcraft, Maria Mendez,
Aldo Rodriguez, Jay Brickman, Bruce Harland, Steve Huff,
Nate Asplund, and Lynn Driskell

While in Cuba, we traveled approximately twelve hundred
miles (wide open) in these two vans.

Grain facility

The US Interests Section ran an electronic ticker criticizing Cuba, and the Cuban government placed the flags to obscure the view.

Jay speaking at the US-Cuba Conference

At the conference with Dr. Gamble, where Cuba accepted the import of poultry from Alabama. There was a ban on US poultry due to the avian flu.

*Former Alabama Agricultural Commissioner Ron Sparks, center,
and the Alabama delegation*

With Ramon Castro Ruz.

Our taxi. Oops, a flat tire!

Maria visiting a Cuban family

Faces of Cuba

8

Passion, Persistence, and Patience

In 1998, Pope John Paul II became the first pontiff ever to visit Cuba. Excitement surrounded his visit, which seemed to exemplify openness on the part of the Catholic Church and support for Cuba's fuller participation in the world. In an address on his arrival on January 21, the Holy Father spoke of both distant and recent history.

> *Arriving on this island, where the cross of Christ was raised over five hundred years ago—the same cross zealously treasured today in the parish church of Baracoa, in the extreme eastern part of the country—I greet everyone with warm affection. This happy and long-awaited day has finally arrived, and I am able to answer the invitation, which the Cuban bishops made a long time ago, and which the president of the republic had also made and personally reiterated on the occasion of his visit to the Vatican in November 1996.*[1]

Fidel Castro was educated at the Belen Jesuit School. He declared Cuba an atheist state after he took power in 1959, but in 1992, the commitment to atheism was dropped from Cuba's constitution. Ahead of the Pope's five-day visit, Christmas was reinstated as an official holiday. If the church was showing flexibility, so was Castro.

Pope John Paul spoke directly of openness. "May Cuba, with all its magnificent potential, open itself up to the world, and may the world open itself up to Cuba, so that this people, which is working to make progress, and which longs for concord and peace, may look to the future with hope."

His message was clearer yet in his farewell address in Havana on January 25.

In our day, no nation can live in isolation. The Cuban people, therefore, cannot be denied the contacts with other peoples necessary for economic, social, and cultural development, especially when the imposed isolation strikes the population indiscriminately, making it ever more difficult for the weakest to enjoy the bare essentials of decent living, things such as food, health, and education. All can and should take practical steps to bring about changes in this regard.

He called on nations sharing a Christian heritage to "join efforts and overcome obstacles" so that the Cuban people could benefit from "international relations, which promote the common good." And he observed that some of their difficulties derived from "oppressive economic measures—unjust and ethically unacceptable—imposed from outside the country." Pope John Paul could hardly have offered a clearer critique of the embargo. Besides condemning US attempts to isolate Cuba, he also called for reform in Cuba, including the release of political prisoners.[2]

The message would be echoed by Pope Benedict XVI on a three-day visit to Cuba in 2012. President Raúl Castro welcomed him to the eastern city of Santiago. "The pontiff said he had come as a pilgrim of charity, and would pray for peace, liberty, and reconciliation. He also expressed sympathy for the 'just aspirations' of all Cuban people, wherever they were."[3] That, of course, would include Miami.

Pope Francis played a major role in bringing the two adversaries together. The Vatican hosted delegations from both the United States and Cuba in October 2014 and used its good offices to facilitate the dialogue that made the changes in Cuban policy possible.

The Vatican's Secretariat of State communicated to the world Pope Francis's congratulations to President Barack Obama and President Raúl Castro for the historic decision by both governments to establish diplomatic relations with the aim of overcoming the difficulties between the two countries.

Jay: Pope John Paul's visit, for me, was a clear indication that there could be changes in US-Cuba relations. After his visit, I felt it was time to take another look at doing business in Cuba. This was the spark that moved the opening of the shipping service in 2001, along with the passing of the Trade Sanctions Reform Act 2000.

Now I constantly receive calls saying, "I want to do business in Cuba." Though it sounds like a broken record, I always ask, "Do you have the passion, patience, and persistence to approach this project?" If you represent a business, then the question also applies to the business you represent. Changes will come, but more slowly than many would like, and the Cuban government will continue to control Cuba's economic activities. *Cuba no es facil.* During my career I have been privileged to live and work in many countries, mostly in the Americas, and I can say, without hesitation, that even with the new changes in policy between the two countries, working in Cuba is like working in a truly different world.

Let me start with passion. If you or the organization you represent doesn't really want to do business in Cuba, you won't. It's that simple. Some people in the past have viewed Cuba as the "forbidden fruit"—they just wanted to travel and do business there because they couldn't. They quickly found out that it is not worth the trouble or money. The cost in time is too great, and the rewards in the short-term are too small. Little by little, that will change.

Both you and your company have to want to do business in Cuba. At the same time, you have to be realistic about whether Cuba wants to do business with you. Cuba needs all kinds of goods and services, but because of US-government legal constraints, this will not be possible immediately. Keep in mind that Cuba has concerns about depending too much on the US market, and economically Cuba is still a limited market. Over time that will change, but if you don't have the passion, persistence, and patience to stick with it, you will quickly get frustrated.

Maria: Like Jay, I receive at least one call a day about how to do business in Cuba, and like him, I agree that it's a process all its own. I too have lived in many countries, and my career has always been focused in the Americas. From the day I left my beloved homeland in August 1961, Cuba has remained an integral part of my life. I'm neither from there nor from here, but a creature of both places. As Cubans say of the exiles who come and visit the island, *de gusana a mariposa*; I left Cuba as a worm, and now I return as a butterfly. In the United States, I'm seen as just another Hispanic, as most people don't take my Cuban heritage into account. The common-language factor fails to account for different foods, histories, and ethnic backgrounds. *Yo soy Cubana*. I am Cuban.

Many in the exile community consider me a traitor for vocalizing my opposition to a senseless embargo. Numerous Cuban Americans cannot let go of the past and accept the simple fact that a revolution did take place. Our hatred is so great that we are blinded.

I have been actively involved in the Cuba issue in some fashion since 1972, when my passion for Cuba flourished while I was attending the University of Florida. I'm a firm believer that the Cuban people in Cuba will determine their destiny, not the exile community in Miami. In many cases, exiles are out of touch with the realities faced by the average Cuban, *el cubano de a pie*.[4] Most exiles have not traveled to the island to see for themselves what life there is like. To this day, when a Cuban American mentions doing away with the embargo or speaks of a presidential mandate for normalized relations, the ultraright in South Florida automatically rejects the speaker as a traitor and communist.

I'm neither a traitor nor a communist, but a Cuban who loves her country, who has accepted that a revolution did happen, and who truly believes that we must move forward and ask what we have accomplished in the past fifty-plus years. I have witnessed firsthand the changes that trade and commerce have brought to Vietnam. Why not apply the same policy to Cuba? And I have been applying passion, persistence, and patience since the day I left Cuba.

Jay: Why Cuba? Passion is something that matters greatly to me. During the forty-something years that I have spent working in Latin America, Cuba has always been present. Whether it was Fidel standing up to the "Yankees," Telmex TV ads about the Helms-Burton law, long discussions about votes in the United Nations, or the many business discussions in countries already trading with the island, Cuba was always "there."

My passion has been a simple one. I think the United States needs to have better relations with Latin America. I am convinced that this will help improve those relationships. American business has blazed the trail and can continue to do so. In the case of Cuba, where there still isn't a smooth flow of commerce, the American business community has the opportunity to lay the groundwork for mutual cooperation and trust. Cuba has an important role to play in this as well.

Maria: If our policy is to continue reaching out to the Cuban people in support of their desire for self-determination, why are some in Congress so adamant about not lifting the embargo? I'm driven by our government's mistrust of others governing themselves, regardless of whether we approve of the path they want to take.

For a number of countries—Argentina, Nicaragua, Ecuador, Venezuela, Bolivia, , Brazil—the embargo has served as a wedge with which to antagonize the United States and alienate its supporters. In reality, the embargo has helped prop up the rule of Castro. The Obama administration began to chip away at it, and Congress is concerned this might be a one-sided deal, which favors Cuba's interest over those of the US. The reality still exists that only Congress can end the five-decade embargo.

Brazil's former president and Latin America's leading statesman Luis Inacio Lula da Silva urged President Barack Obama in 2009, at the beginning of his administration, to end the embargo. Lula correctly identified our policy toward Cuba as the main stumbling block for renewed US ties with Latin America, as it has been from the start of the Castro regime.

Jay: Let me share an experience that illustrates the importance of persistence. In 1978, Tom Crowley Sr., the owner of Crowley Maritime Corporation, questioned whether Crowley Maritime should be looking at Cuba. His interest was purely commercial, not political. His curiosity was sparked by the Carter Administration seemingly changing US policy toward Cuba, which seemed to be opening up. Tom's feeling was that if trade opened with Cuba, this would offer an opportunity for the liner-shipping service that he was constructing in Central America and the Caribbean. In looking at the Crowley Maritime shipping network, Cuba was either in the way or on the way.

We began to study the possibility of serving Cuba in 1978. Tom was fully aware that we could not do business there, but he was curious about Cuba. Because of his interest, I made a first trip to Cuba in 1978. My visit was coordinated by Kirby Jones, president of Alamar Associates. A few years earlier Kirby had begun to cooperate with the Cuban government in setting up business trips to Cuba.

Although structured, the trip was fascinating and provided me with tremendous insight into the potential of the Cuban market. It also made me question the relationship between Cuba and the United States. The more I looked into and analyzed the relationship between the two countries, the more questions I had. My persistence to work in matters relating to Cuba was planted at this point.

While moving with Crowley from Jacksonville, Florida; to San Juan, Puerto Rico; and then to Caracas; New York; New Orleans; Mexico; and finally Miami; I continued to maintain old contacts and develop new ones in Cuba. As I moved from one assignment to another, I cleaned out numerous files, but I always kept my Cuban files.

In 1991, I traveled again to Cuba, this time alone. Cuba was facing "*El Período Especial*."[5] The Soviet Union had collapsed, and the Cuban economy had disintegrated. During this time, Cuba lost 80 percent of its imports and 80 percent of its exports. Its gross domestic product dropped by 34 percent. Food and medicine imports practically came to a standstill. Perhaps most immediately impactful was the loss of nearly all oil imports from the USSR; Cuba's oil imports dropped to 10 percent of pre-1990 amounts.[6] All this adversity never dulled my enthusiasm.

This trip (almost fourteen years after the first—it was hard to believe) was sponsored by Crowley's Venezuelan partner, and the purpose was to explore the possibility of the Venezuelan partner doing business in Cuba. The US restrictions clearly did not permit Crowley to do business there. The challenge was to continue to present Crowley in a positive way to the Cuban government and at the same time maintain Crowley's interest in a long-range project and begin laying the groundwork for how to work with the US government to permit a vessel to trade with Cuba.

We learned three lessons at this juncture: if your company has an interest in Cuba, be sure to keep the apparent opportunity in perspective; the corporate view has to be for the long run; and make sure you have a number of other projects going at the same time. The unspoken fourth lesson was to apply a great deal of patience.

Maria: If there is something I do not have, it's patience, but when dealing with Cuba, I have a lot of passion and persistence. During this time, I was visiting a dear friend in Miami, Elsita Perez. She was like a mother to me, a Cuban exile who came to the United States in 1961. She was in her late eighties when I visited and invited her to come shopping with me at Wal-Mart.

We went to every single aisle, loading two carts full of merchandise When we got to the checkout line, I placed the items on the belt but then mentioned to the poor checkout clerk, "Oops, I can't buy this. It's made in China." Not one single item on those carts was made anywhere else.

The people behind me and the clerk were about to explode when I asked, "Are you all Cuban?"

One woman said, "Who in Westchester is not a Cuban?"

With a big smile on my face, I calmly asked my key question. "How can I buy from and support trade with China, when we cannot trade with Cuba? Please tell me the difference."

I was proud of myself that day; I made my point. I would like to know how many items from China or Vietnam those Florida legislators and Cuban American politicians have in their homes and offices. Made in China, made in China, made in China.

My dear friend Elsita did not always agree with my point of view, and sadly, she passed away a year later, but that day at Wal-Mart she laughed so hard that it brought tears to her eyes. After all the years of patience, for once I felt I had the last laugh.

Let's examine some details from an official description of the Chinese government, according to the CIA's *The World Factbook*:[7]

Executive branch:

Chief of state: president
Cabinet: State Council appointed by National People's Congress

Legislative branch:

Unicameral National People's Congress

Judicial branch:

Judge selection and term of office: chief justice appointed by the National People's Congress; term limited to two consecutive five-year terms; other justices and judges nominated by the chief justice and appointed by the Standing Committee of the National People's Congress

Political parties and leaders:

Chinese Communist Party or CCP
Eight nominally independent small parties ultimately controlled by the CCP

Political pressure groups and leaders:

No substantial political opposition groups exist

The description applies to Vietnam as well as Cuba. Why can we not accept the Cuban government structure as it is?

Jay: In 1998, it became obvious that things really were changing. By this time, Maria and I had a steady stream of communication. Our normal form of working together is competitive. We constantly push each other to see who knows what first. As a team, we became known as Piedra (her maiden name) and Ladrillo: Stone and Brick. We joked about it with some of the Cuban officials, suggesting they name an avenue *Piedra y Ladrillo*.

As mentioned, Pope John Paul's historic visit to Cuba in January 1998 was significant. Welcomed by Fidel Castro, the Pope also had some strong words for him—what a *New York Times* reporter described as a "ringing call for pluralism." The exercise of freedom of conscience was "the basis and foundation of all other human rights," said John Paul. "A modern state cannot make atheism or religion one of its political ordinances."[8] As we have seen in his farewell speech, the pope condemned the economic embargo. In trying to be objective, we should note that Castro urged the Cuban population to attend the papal mass, if not out of conviction, at least out of respect. Pope John Paul's visit began to change attitudes on both sides.

Maria: I have always said that my faith is what keeps me going. As a Catholic, for me, the Pope's visit made a tremendous impact, in particular his message about Cuba opening itself to the world so as to "look to the future with hope." The Pope's visit was unforgettable, a spiritual reawakening, a time for social and cultural reconciliation for Cuba and the United States.

Jay: At the same time, discussions on limited trade with Cuba in the Senate and in the House were gaining support. Farm groups were uniting to support trade with Cuba. The reasons were economic. The US farm sector was facing falling agricultural exports and declining commodity prices. This effort resulted in including Cuba in the Trade Sanction Reform and Export Enhancement Act of 2000 (TSRA).

In June 1998, I spoke with Crowley's attorney in Washington, DC. We discussed what was happening and came to the conclusion that if goods were to move, there had to be a way to move them. We used the logic that air traffic was permitted between the United States and Cuba, and charter flights were permitted to carry the passengers. Therefore, if cargo was going to be permitted to move under TSRA, ships should be permitted to operate.

Based on this, we approached the Office of Foreign Assets Control and the Department of Commerce to discuss what licenses had to be issued to permit necessary travel for vessels to operate between the United States and Cuba.

By the beginning of 2001, we had the needed licenses, we had permission from the Cuban government to dock, and TSRA was in place. In March 2001, former vice president Carlos Lage announced that he did not have a problem with Crowley calling on Cuba—but that Cuba "would not buy even an aspirin from the United States."[9] A number of possible shippers advised us that they were prepared to ship goods to Cuba and that these shipments would be paid for out of private funds. We decided to test the waters, and we set up a first sailing to Cuba.

Now all we needed was the cargo. This turned out to be a fatal flaw. For the first vessel, in spite of much interest, there were only a few containers booked, and we received a booking to carry cargo for the US Interests Section in Cuba (a limited diplomatic presence, within the Swiss Embassy). Our reasoning was that this cargo normally moved to Cuba via a third country, but we had permission from both countries to carry cargo to Cuba, and we had a port agent in Cuba, so we agreed to carry this cargo. A Crowley executive held a press conference announcing the opening of the Cuban service. On April 20, 2001, we sailed from Jacksonville, Florida. The vice president for operations Mike Hopkins and I flew to Havana to receive the vessel. We were ready to make history!

Maria: Jay and I had worked for so long on this endeavor, and finally the day was upon us. While I was employed at the Jacksonville Port Authority, Crowley had been my customer, and over the years, I had introduced several of their key executives to the personnel at the Cuban Interests Section. I had also invited former chief of mission Fernando Ramirez Estenoz, First Secretary Gustavo Machin, and Consul Luis Molina to visit Jacksonville to tour the port and meet several of the local business and political leaders. It was then that I experienced the first wave of backlash from the Cuban American community.

At least twice a year, the chief of mission in Washington invited a group of Cuban Americans to meet at his residence and openly discuss issues pertaining to the Cuban exile community. I was impressed that they wanted to listen to and engage in dialogue with parties such as me. I want to be clear that at no point did they criticize our efforts or try to persuade us to the contrary. On one of their visits to Jacksonville, I had arranged a dinner with other Cuban Americans. Discussions grew hot, but as we went back and forth, we agreed on one profitable business: burial in Cuba of Cubans who die in exile.

Jay: Four hours before the arrival of the vessel, our agent Jorge Pascual received a call and said we had to depart immediately to attend a meeting. Jorge is a bear of a guy, about six feet, three inches tall and 250 pounds, and the bear was pale. As we departed, I asked him if there was a problem. He said he didn't know. I asked where we were going. To the Mambisa shipping agency, he replied. Why? He didn't know. I advised Mike, "We've got a problem, but I don't know what it is."

Arriving at the Mambisa office, we went into Eduardo Denis's conference room. Eduardo, normally jovial, was superserious.

"Hi, Eduardo, what's happening?"

"Hi, Jay, Mike, Jorge. Please have a seat."

Mike excused himself to go to the restroom, and I asked Eduardo if we could see what was up.

"No, Jay. Let's wait so that we can all review this."

When Mike returned to the conference room, Eduardo advised us that he had instructions to read us a message.

"*Se ha decidido por nuestro gobierno no aceptar la descarga de la mercancia mientras no haya reciprocidad o sea mientras que el gobierno de los Estados Unidos no permita que los buques Cubanos pueden hacer lo mismo en puertos Norte Americanos.*" [Our government has decided not to permit the unloading of merchandise while there is no reciprocal agreement with the United States allowing Cuban vessels to carry the same merchandise in US ports.]

"Eduardo, what is this?" I asked. "We have worked together for a long time on this service. What happened?"

"Would you like me to read the message again?" asked Eduardo. He did so.

"OK, so that I am clear," I concluded, "this ship we have that is four hours outside of port cannot dock in Havana. Is that correct?"

"Jay, if you want to dock the vessel, we certainly will not refuse that. But you can't unload the cargo."

"But, Eduardo, if we can't unload, why dock?"

"Jay, that is your decision."

I asked Eduardo if I could have a copy of the message. He said no.

Maria: The press kept calling for a statement from the port. I talked to our public-relations manager who said, "Not a word! This is Crowley's call."

In the meantime, I called Secretary Gustavo Machin of the Cuban Interests Section, and in less than an hour, he was on a plane headed to Jacksonville, Fl. I drove to the airport and picked him up, and we headed directly to Crowley's local office, In the mean time Jay and Mike Hopkins, who where in Havana tried to make sense of what was happening in Cuba. .

Gustavo met in private with Crowley's upper management, as I waited outside. The situation was critical. Gustavo made it very clear to me on his way back to the airport that under no circumstances could Crowley transport cargo destined for the US Interests Section. "Gustavo reiterated thatCuba had not closed its door, and hope was not lost to transport other cargoes.

Jay: We all agreed that there was nothing more we could do at Mambisa. Jorge dropped us off at the hotel. Mike and I needed to speak with Tom Crowley. I talked with Tom, and we decided that nothing had happened. The situation was simply that the vessel would not dock in Havana, and there had been a change in route.

Cargo aside, the real business of the day was navigating our way toward ease for all the players. We later learned that the Cuban government had been highly concerned about how Crowley would react to the snag, and by not reacting, we had paved the road for continued relations. We learned some important lessons that day.

1. Ask before you act. In dealing with governments, if there is a gray area, it is better to ask. It may take a while to get an answer, and you may not like the answer you get—but asking is better. In addition there is always the danger that you don't know what you don't know.

2. Build confidence. Open relations and confidence building are essential. There were two errors on the first vessel. First, the press release was not welcomed by Cuba. It gave the impression that commercial relations between Cuba and the United States were in good condition. Second, it caused Fidel Castro to ask what was on the vessel. That brought attention to the US Interests Section cargo. We later learned that such cargo was supposed to move under a bilateral agreement between the two governments, and shipping it directly was in violation of that agreement. This illustrates that what you don't know can hurt you. Because of the relations we had built with the Cuban government, I think they understood that we had acted in good faith, and consequently, they granted us a meeting in June 2001 to review what could be done.

3. Correct errors. Once we understood Cuba's concern about the control of the flow of cargo, we worked with the Cuban officials to set up a system to assure that this mistake would not be repeated. The system we developed jointly set up the infrastructure to permit the movement of containerized cargo from the United States to Cuba.

Every time I grow discouraged about a project in Cuba, a dear friend reminds me, "Brickman, *todavia no hay aprendido paciencia*?" You still have not learned patience?

Following the June meeting, I received a call from Comercio Exterior in Havana that I should come to Cuba. They wanted to bring cargo from the United States. My first concern was how to obtain a business visa in Venezuela, where I was at the time. MINCEX immediately arranged with the Cuban Embassy in Caracas to issue the visa. At the same time, they worked with the Cuban Interests Section in Washington to issue a visa to Rinus Schepen, at the time Senior Vice President of Crowley Liner Services, to come to Havana from Jacksonville.

We all got together on November 22, 2001—Thanksgiving—and signed the first contract with a government entity we did not know, Alimport, and with a gentleman we had never met named Pedro Alvarez. Together we programmed the call of the first vessel from the United States to Cuba in more than forty years.

We feel it is important to express our gratitude to those individuals in Cuba and the US government who made this historic event possible, in particular to two special women at Comercio Exterior who were responsible for North America. We were all exhilarated to pull off that first ship's call.

In our case, the mode of expanding interchange with Cuba involved efforts to resume shipping, certainly among the more intricate aspects of the embargo and arguably among the more urgent. As we are maritime trade professionals, that was where we found the opportunity to improve the two countries' relations. We are proud of that success. Officials in the United States and Cuba made it happen, but the business community was the spearhead.

Not the least of what this reveals is that many other possible dimensions exist for such endeavors. A second arena in which we have tried to encourage rapprochement is academia. Would it make sense for the University of Texas to ignore the state's proximity to and relationship with Mexico? Obviously not. It is far more illuminating, useful, and rewarding to explore and celebrate this close connection. Does it make sense for Florida's flagship university, the University of Florida, to face difficulty in openly discussing US-Cuban relations? Cuba is a near neighbor.

The alumni of the Latin American Studies program at the University of Florida, of which I am a member, strongly believe that the university needs to be the best-informed and most influential group on the US-Cuba horizon. Yet it has traditionally had little exposure to, or involvement in, Cuban matters. You can feel the Miami Mania when you visit the University of Florida, and other Florida educational institueions. Miami Mania produces the state laws challenging the US Constitution and causes universities' apprehension in considering a balanced program of Cuban studies for fear of losing their state funding. We are encouraged by lone-wolf professors who keep trying to nudge the university toward more involvement in Cuban studies, and times are changing. Although lone-wolf professors run into state politics at every turn, they keep trying to nudge.

Meetings have begun; travel to Cuba is under way, which will start to engage the University of Florida and Cubans with the effort; and grant applications to support the research are in process. The university appears to be poised for some of the barriers to start coming down. It's another classic instance of needing extra doses of passion, persistence, and patience to keep the project moving along.

Maria: The University of Alabama has been extremely aggressive in its relations with the University of Havana. The Alabama-Cuba Initiative has brought UA and Cuban educators together to establish opportunities for graduate-student research, teaching, and formal course work for undergraduate students at Cuban academic institutions and has also allowed Cuban educators to come to UA for collaborative work.[10] As described in the chapter that follows, professors from Auburn University played a key role, in explainig the protocols used in controling the avian flu that began in 2003. In June 2015 Auburn University, The State of Alabama, the Alabama Departemnt of Agriculture and Industries, the Port Alabama Port Authority and Crowley Maritime continue to play a key role in reasuring the safety of Alabama poultry production is safe.

Jay: In addition to Florida, I have been fortunate to work with one of the "granddaddy" programs in Cuban Studies. For years, the David Rockefeller School of Latin American Studies has had student exchange and visiting scholar programs. Being an eminent private university does have some advantages!

9

Politics and *Pollos*

The first US food product to arrive in Cuba in 2001 was poultry. The *Crowley Express* arrived a little after noon on December 16, while the *Mazatlan* arrived in Havana at about four o'clock with a load of corn. Word came that the captain of the *Express* had advised the *Mazatlan* that he was behind on his schedule and would arrive later in Havana, and in the meantime, he sped up—but that is a story for another time. The first product to arrive in Cuba was, indeed, poultry aboard the *Crowley Express*.

Since that first vessel on December 16, 2001, the US poultry industry has shipped almost a billion dollars' worth of poultry to Cuba. There are some good reasons for the industry's success. First, the United States has an efficient and internationally competitive poultry industry. Second, the US and Cuban markets are complementary: US consumers prefer chicken breasts, while the Cuban preference is leg quarters. Last, the logistics of shipping from the United States facilitate a smooth and economical flow of product to Cuba.

Even with all these advantages, the poultry industry faced two significant challenges in 2004. Avian flu had a devastating impact on the industry in the latter part of 2003 and early 2004. Countries across the world were canceling US poultry orders. Cuba was one of the countries that announced a ban. Poultry was an important component in maintaining a regular ship call on Havana, and it was also paramount to the agricultural sector in Alabama and other states.

Avian flu was the problem; politics hindered a resolution to the problem. There was, and is, a great relationship between the US poultry industry and Cuba, but the Cuban government had serious concerns about the peril of importing US chickens.

The Animal and Plant Health Inspection Service (APHIS) of the US Department of Agriculture and the Veterinarian Department of the Cuban government were in communication, but politically, the Cuban officials wanted more. They wanted a ranking member of APHIS to come to Cuba. Today such a trip might be difficult; in 2004 it was not politically feasible. In effect, Cuba was saying that it did not have sufficient information to lift the ban, and APHIS said it was giving all the information available, but that a representative could not come to Cuba. At the same time, Cuba could not obtain visas to send representatives to the United States. We had a stalemate.

Jay: Maria Conchita and I met with Alimport and asked what needed to be done to permit the resumption of trade. The answer was to have the USDA send the proper representative to Cuba. We said that simply would not happen. After this initial meeting with Alimport, we consulted with the Alabama Department of Agriculture, under the direction, at the time, of Commissioner Ron Sparks. We asked if the State was interested and able to send a qualified person to Cuba to discuss the protocols that were in place to control the infected poultry.

The reply was promising. Poultry represented the second-largest agricultural product in Alabama, and there was a great interest in protecting its position in the Cuban market. And at Auburn University, Alabama had two of the top experts in the country on the protocols for controlling avian flu. The state of Alabama was ready and willing to send these two experts to Cuba. We immediately called Dr. John Gamble, agricultural economic administrator, who said, "We have the two top experts in the nation, and they will be on the next flight to Cuba."

In March 2004, they went to Cuba and met with Cuban government officials. Without the continued communications between APHIS and the Cuban government, the lifting of the ban would have taken much longer, but the two experts from Alabama gave credibility to the conversation. They were a "tipping point," and the poultry began to move.

Maria: With this problem resolved, we approached the 2004 International Trade Fair in Havana with a great deal of enthusiasm about improved relations between the United States and Cuba. From a business and political point of view, things seemed to be improving. The trade from the United States was growing; business cooperation with both the US and Cuban governments was becoming more routine; and every once in a while, it seemed that relations between the two governments were even improving.

As the trade grew, so did the number of visitors from the United States: US congressional representatives, senators, governors, state agricultural commissioners, and presidents of the various trade associations such as the poultry organization and the wheat and rice growers. As an importing country, Cuba had moved from zero to being the twenty-third largest importer of agricultural products from the United States.

Of course, everyone wanted to be able to claim to have met Fidel Castro and to have been in close proximity to the Comandante.[1] Delegates all wanted to talk about their appointment with Pedro Alvarez, the former president of Alimport. Pedro signed the contracts. Meeting the man behind the name gave the proceedings and documents fuller reality.

So everyone was ready for the November 2004 trade fair. Products were bought, business was growing, and all the travelers would have a story to tell about their trip to Cuba.

Jay: By the second day of the trade fair, rumors were rampant. Shippers asked me what I knew about the US Treasury's Office of Foreign Assets Control (OFAC) stopping the banking transactions to transfer funds from foreign banks to US sellers.

One thing you learn in international business is that rumors, especially negative ones, can spread like wildfire. The "rule of ten" applies—count to ten and reappraise what you have heard. Having done that, we found that not only did the rumors not disappear, but shippers began to seek assurances that the goods they had in the port of Havana were secure, that the

Cuban government would not try to remove these goods from the port until they were released, and that the shippers were not violating any US laws. From a logistical point of view, a perfect storm was brewing.

- The New Year's cargo was flowing from the United States to Cuba.
- Cargo was being manufactured or slaughtered for delivery.
- Cargo was in warehouses with appointments to load.
- Cargo was in port awaiting the next vessel.
- Cargo was onboard vessels moving toward Havana.
- Cargo was in Havana to supply the population for the New Year.

All this implied cost, cost, and more cost, and the pressure was increasing on the executives, myself included, who had convinced their companies to be involved in the Cuban venture.

Underlying the situation was the question the various suppliers had about whether they were doing something illegal. The rules of the game were changing, and there was a real danger that all involved would suffer financial losses. We were trying to obtain as much information as possible for our US customers and for Alimport while at the fair in Havana. We did not have good communications with the United States from the island, and it was the peak trading season, before Thanksgiving.

We all wondered why this was happening after three years of growing trade that had produced more than $750 million in purchases in the United States. In retrospect, it was happening specifically because the trade was growing.

Maria: I was disillusioned with the Bush Administration and the lack of support the business community at the fair received from the chief of mission to the US Interests Section, James Cason. (Cuba and the United States, of course, had no embassies on each other's terrain, and in the absence of embassies, the Interests Section was where the buck stopped.) He discouraged the businesses that attended the fair from engaging in any commercial transactions with Alimport. Meanwhile, as a Cuban American, I had circulated and talked to people and saw for myself how the poultry was reaching the general population. I had hoped for better understanding from the United States, but unfortunately that was not to be.

It is important to examine Cuba's point of view during this critical period. The growth in trade attracted more and more interested business parties in the United States, to the degree that they were having an impact on Cuba policy in Congress. At the end of 2004, the House of Representatives passed an amendment favoring the elimination of travel restrictions to Cuba. The increase in trade plus the more conciliatory attitude in the House were negatively received by the Bush Administration and by the PAC in Miami. This reaction played an important role in assuring that the travel amendment was not passed in the Senate, and it complicated future trade terms.

Jay: Just as US businesses were preparing for new contracts at the fair, the Office of Foreign Assets Control (OFAC) launched a new offensive on the interpretation of advance payments. Cuba was concerned about paying for products before they were shipped from the United States. The concern was that such goods could be considered Cuban government property and consequently might be subject to confiscation in the United States.

OFAC's action in November 2004 endangered the continuation of trade, and it threatened to create additional problems between the two countries. The first impact was that money paid by Cuba was not permitted to transfer from foreign banks to US banks. The suppliers could not receive their payments, and to make matters worse, break-bulk vessels with grain and containerized cargo, for which Cuba had paid, could not be unloaded into, or dispatched from, Cuban ports.

Maria: The former president of Alimport, Pedro Alvarez, called Jay and me into his office and delivered a strong and direct message. He had received a call from Fidel Castro asking what was happening and advising him that Cuban citizens were complaining about not receiving products for Christmas and New Year. Keep in mind that grapes are a must for the Cuban people in their New Year celebration. Castro had been highly critical of the way Alvarez was handling the delicate state of affairs. He informed us that according to Castro's directives, "the US government had licensed the sale and export of agricultural products and now was breaking that agreement; the Cubans had no choice but to cancel all of our orders."

Jay: We had to go back to the rule of ten. Count slowly, take out all the emotion, and look pragmatically at what needed to be done. First, we needed to obtain assurance from the Cuban government on two items. Could they assure us that the cargo in Cuban ports would not be removed before it was given a release by the suppliers, whose payments were frozen by OFAC? Alimport's answer was yes. They said the law stated that they could not remove the cargo until it was properly released, and they would respect the law.

Second, Cuban customs advised that this cargo had not cleared customs in Cuba and that it could be returned to the United States. Next we had to consult with US Customs to see if the cargo would be permitted to be returned to the United States. The response was that if the cargo was still effectively in international transit, it could be returned to the United States.

Although OFAC's change of interpretation of the terms of trade caused huge problems, both governments were cooperating in order to avoid making the situation worse. Ultimately, OFAC permitted the delivery of the goods that were in transit using the previous interpretation regarding payment.

From the beginning of this situation, I was in constant communication with the former chief of the Cuban Interests Section, Dagoberto Rodriguez; former director of the North America Ministry of Commerce MariLu B'Hamel; and former president of Alimport, Pedro Alvarez. There is no way that I can congratulate them enough for the approach they ultimately took. They stayed calm, protected all their legal commercial agreements, and most important of all, they did not get into tit-for-tat type diplomacy. I'm sure the temptation was there.

Maria: I was extremely impressed by the Cubans who dealt with North America. They had a wealth of knowledge of US law and policy. Ironically, they often wound up telling us, "This cannot be done under US law." I was devastated after personally witnessing how trade with the United States had touched so many ordinary Cubans. The Cuban government never stopped me from taking an unofficial taxi and visiting neighborhoods in Old Havana, Alamar, La Bivora, El Vedado, Guanavacoa, Lawton, and elsewhere.

I made it a point to establish people-to-people contact. Picking homes at random to visit, I found they always had something to offer. We talked for hours about US poultry, how big the chicken legs were, and how the embargo made no sense. I learned about the famous *caldoza*, a Cuban soup to which everyone on the block contributes some vegetable or meat; once it's ready, they hold the equivalent of a block party. The items we were shipping were indeed reaching the Cuban population; yes, some went to tourism, but in order to pay the United States in cash, the Cubans needed a source of revenue. We needed to find a solution, and fast.

Jay: We had to address what would be the solution to maintain ongoing trade. One thing was clear. No one party would find the solution. It was time to circle the wagons. It was imperative to work together with legal counsel, commodity associations, suppliers, and the legislative branch. An alliance was formed that, incredibly, held together until a workable solution was reached on July 29, 2005.

Senator Max Baucus proved to be the key in getting the administration's attention and, ultimately, cooperation. President Bush wanted Senate confirmation of his appointments to the Treasury, and Senator Baucus was withholding that approval. An agreement was reached with OFAC that permitted the use of letters of credit from third countries to pay for shipments from the United States.

At the conclusion of this arduous process, Senator Baucus said, "The fact remains, however, that this Treasury rule is still in place, and as long as it is, we'll never be able to realize the full potential of the Cuban market. I remain 100 percent committed to overturning this rule fully, and I will work hard to get Congress to send legislation to the President's desk [that] this session that will do just that."[2] In spite of the senator's best effort, that legislation is still pending. It is truly time for a change in policy.

Anya Landau, who was on Senator Baucus's Finance Committee, perhaps best summed up what we accomplished after a lot of tiring days and sleepless nights. In her closing e-mail to all, she wrote, "Your kind message nearly brings tears (all right, of exhaustion as much as joy) to my eyes! It definitely was like rolling the boulder up the hill! Brian and I were just so grateful that you guys stuck with us, didn't give up, worked tirelessly into the nights and mornings to explain, to return to the drawing board again and again, and miracles of miracles, strike a deal."

Some of the lessons we learned from all this were the following:

- Stay cool. Even at the sessions that lasted all night, there was nothing to be gained by adding emotion to an already volatile situation.
- Alliances are essential. Obtaining clarification of a change in a US policy that is politically motivated is not easy. There is a great deal of justified criticism of PACs, lobbyists, and lawmakers, but without them, it is impossible to obtain the support needed to open the lines of communication.
- These processes take time. If you are not prepared to invest time and patience in the process, you should not attempt to make the changes.
- Communication is key. Lines of communication must be kept open with all parties involved.

What were the unintended consequences of this? First, the process of working together formed a closer alliance of the companies and gave them a fuller understanding of the Cuban position. Second, the new OFAC rules enabled the Cuban government to save millions of dollars that were being spent on demurrage and detention.

There was a third consequence, perhaps unintended. This event reinforced Cuba's reluctance to broaden trade. For example, under TSRA Cuba could buy medicine and medical equipment and supplies from the United States. But one of the greatest concerns in Cuba is that the United States might arbitrarily cut off the flow of these essential commodities.

The year 2008 would prove to be the period of peak trading between Cuba and the United States. The Cuban government statement about the 2008 US trade read, "In 2008, there was a record level of imports by Alimport from the United States. Alimport bought more than $800 million in US products. This important figure undoubtedly generated thousands of jobs in the United States for the agricultural sector, transportation companies, ports, and other sectors." Their report did not say so, but a lot of those jobs were probably in Florida.[3]

Besides proximity to market, one of the reasons why Cuba was purchasing agricultural goods from the United States was to influence change in US policy regarding direct banking, credit, and free flow of travel. As result of not achieving its goal, Cuba changed its trade policy toward the United States, and US exports have not recovered to 2008 volumes. With the announcement on December 17, 2014, there will again be growth in trade between the two countries. Almost surely, there will again be conflicts and misunderstandings.

After the December 17th announcement subsequent executive actions taken by the Obama Administration, it was assumed that there would be an increase in the trade between the two countries. To support the initiative taken by President Obama and President Castro, there is a great deal of activity in the US Congress and the private sector in the US is reaching out more than ever to both the government and private sector in Cuba. OFAC has even changed the cash in advance rule that we spoke of previously. However, pollos have again become an area of concern.

In June of 2015, Cuba announced a "commercial" decision to not buy poultry in the United States at least during the period of June to September. This was a shock to the industry that had become the backbone of trade from the United States to Cuba. It was also a setback for the nascent private sector which depends on reliable transportation.

In trying to resolve this situation, we have some lessons learned in this book. First the "rule of ten". Count slowly, one, two …Secondly, we again are pulling together an alliance. The purpose of the alliance is to assure that poultry is available at very competitive commercial prices and that there is not a danger of contracting Avian Flu from US poultry originating in Alabama and Georgia. These two states are the largest poultry producing states in the United States. The State of Alabama along with Crowley has taken on a pro-active role in assuring good communications and technical support. All involved are using "passion, patience and persistence".

Lessons learned? Again, stay cool, alliances are essential, processes take time and good communications is key. As they say in Cuba, "no es facil".

10

Y Cuba Que?

"**H**uman rights should remain the measure of US policy toward Cuba," proclaimed the *Miami Herald* in an editorial in early 2014. "Not only is there no sign that the Castro regime is interested in any sort of dialogue or negotiation over its despotic policies, but rather the opposite."[1]

The piece notes that there is movement, or at least the "start of a conversation," in the European Union and among Americans about policy toward Cuba. It cites a Pew poll indicating that majorities in the United States, even among Cuban Americans, favor "a thaw in relations." It notes the claim made by those wanting the embargo lifted: "the failure to make an impact on Cuba's behavior after all these decades is proof that the embargo doesn't work."

But the *Herald* also notes that countries fielding a more "flexible and engaging policy toward Cuba haven't made a difference either." And the editorial concludes as it begins: "Cuba's dismal human rights record should be the foremost consideration in any domestic dialogue about US policy." This is classic Miami Mania speaking. Never mind that the policy is not working. We will not change it unless the Cubans clean up their act.

Quite often in discussions about normalizing relations with Cuba, it is mentioned that the United States has normal diplomatic relations with China and Vietnam, and more recently with Myanmar. *Y Cuba que?* What about Cuba?

The three Asian countries all have communist histories and governments that routinely violate human rights. Are they different from Cuba because they are far away? Until now, US policy toward Cuba has remained rooted in an approach devised at the height of the Cold War. We certainly support improvement of human rights for everyone, but in relation to politics between nations, we have to recognize the sovereignty of each country.

It comes down to this: changes in policy occur only when there are compelling reasons for change. A brief look at some of the background to the US approach to normalizing diplomatic relations with Myanmar, Vietnam, and China helps shed light on how to build new bridges for the future relationship between the United States and Cuba.

We need to distinguish between trade and normal diplomatic relations. They are not the same thing. There has been limited trade from the United States to Cuba since 2001, but there have not been normal diplomatic relations. The two presidents have taken the first steps to normalization. On the other hand the US Congress needs to abrogate the laws prohibiting free trade, and the Cuban government needs to designate those government and private entities that can participate in trade between Cuba and the US. If Congress approves an ambassador and funds an embassy, we will then have normal diplomatic relations.

China, Vietnam, and Myanmar all have a history of communist or military governments routinely accused of violating human rights. With these three Asian countries, neither trade nor change in government structure has been the reason to normalize diplomatic relations. If that were the case, looking at the trade balances and government structure, we would argue that the United States is a weak negotiator.

In one respect, the Republic of the Union of Myanmar is the case most similar to Cuba. Today the stated US objective is to establish a civilian democratic government based on the rule of law and the protection of basic human rights. But the compelling reason to attempt this is the overarching US policy of trying to stabilize relations in the Far East. The Obama Administration has moved from a reactive "action-for-action" strategy and a skeptical and cautious attitude, toward a more proactive mode in its dealings with the newly created union government and union parliament. The new approach is designed to foster further reforms based on some form of partnership with the union government headed by President Thein Sein.

Normalization of diplomatic relations between the United States and the Socialist Republic of Vietnam occurred in 1995. The compelling reasons for the United States were to locate people who were missing in action or had been prisoners of war (MIAs and POWs); the need for a counterbalance to China to help stabilize the Pacific region; and the effort to find a home for the boat people displaced after the Vietnam War. The Vietnamese wanted war reparations (which they did not get), foreign investment (which they did obtain), and entry into the US markets (which did happen); however, Vietnam did not change its government structure.

China, however, is another story. Just as some domestic interests are opposed to improving relations with Cuba, there was once strong opposition to improving relations with China. There was also a strong Cold War concern about China's geopolitical goals. A 1958 Department of State memorandum offered two basic conclusions regarding the approach to China.

First, the Soviet bloc, of which Communist China was an important part, was engaged in a long-range struggle to destroy the way of life of the free countries.

Second...East Asia was peculiarly vulnerable to the Communist offensive because of the proximity of the free countries of that area to Communist China.

In defining US policy toward China at that time, representatives of the Department of State said, "In the view of the United States, diplomatic recognition is a privilege and not a right. Moreover, the United States considers that diplomatic recognition is an instrument of national policy, which is both its right and its duty to use in the enlightened self-interest of the nation."[2] So what happened to change all this?

Compelling reasons arose on both sides to change their relationship. After the Sino-Soviet border clash in 1969, the People's Republic of China was diplomatically isolated. The Chinese leadership hoped that improved relations with the United States would help counterbalance Soviet power.

The United States, in its Cold War effort, was seeking ways to weaken the Sino-Soviet bloc. Normalization came in 1978 and today seems a distant memory.

Ironically, China's expanding role in the Americas may become a compelling reason to normalize relations with Cuba as a step to improving relations in the Americas. There is concern about Chinese expansion in Asia, and we need to note it in our own neighborhood as well. The Pew Research Center released a study in July 2013 revealing that the Latin American region prefers Chinese influence over US influence, although maintaining strong ties with the United States is still a priority.

The study showed that in Venezuela, which is the recipient of millions in investment and financing from China, 57 percent of respondents see Beijing as a positive influence, and the figure rises to 71 percent when the question involves China's impact on the economy. In comparison, the perception of US influence in Venezuela shows only 29 percent seeing the United States as a positive influence and just 46 percent regarding US influence in Venezuelan economic affairs as positive for the country.

The same study indicates that the most positive view of China's influence in the region is among respondents in Chile (36 percent), Bolivia (31 percent), and Argentina (27 percent), while the United States finds most support in El Salvador (51 percent), Brazil (46 percent), and Mexico (33 percent), and its margins over China are minimal. President Barack Obama traveled to Costa Rica and Mexico in May 2013, declaring that Latin America represents an "opportunity" for the United States. During this trip, he tried to revive the US relationship with the region, which, for the last decade, has generally languished in Washington.

Later that same month, on the heels of President Obama's visit, China's President Xi Jinping toured Costa Rica, Mexico, and Trinidad and Tobago, offering increased Chinese trade and investment in Latin America. Eight months earlier, Chinese commerce minister, Chen Deming, participated in the twenty-fifth session of the China-Cuba Intergovernmental Commission, reaffirming China's commitment to strengthening economic and trade ties. He signed numerous contracts with Cuba spanning twelve sectors, including finance, agriculture, fundamental equipment, seafood, biochemistry, pharmaceuticals, and possible oil resources.

During the session, Chen said, "I hope Chinese investors can visit Cuba. They should take note of the embargo put in place by the United States, and the fact that the market is limited. They should also see Cuba's reforms and the country's huge potential for exploring the market in the Caribbean and Latin American regions."[4] Minister Chen's visit to Cuba in September 2012 was itself a follow-up to a visit to China in July by President Raúl Castro.

Maria: In 1934, the Treaty of Relations between the United States and Cuba was negotiated as a part of the "good neighbor" policy, and most of the Platt Amendment was repealed, meaning that the United States was formally relinquishing its right to intervene in Cuban affairs. Our policy toward Cuba historically remained one of interventions, neglect, and missed opportunities.

Looking at the example of China, several more questions arise. Is Cuba an important part of a struggle to destroy our way of life? Are Latin America and the Caribbean particularly vulnerable to a communist offensive led by Cuba? If neither applies, why is there an embargo in place?

Jay: As we look toward building bridges between the United States and Cuba, what can we learn from what happened in China, Vietnam, and Myanmar?

- Both sides need compelling reasons to normalize diplomatic relations.
- Neither government should have changing the domestic policies of the other government as its primary objective. The Chinese Communist Party continues to govern China, the Vietnamese Communist Party continues to govern Vietnam, and President Thein Sein is still the president of Myanmar.
- US policy toward Cuba is very much like the US policy was toward China in 1958. As discussed earlier in this chapter, the United States had a compelling reason (and opportunity) in 1969 to change its

policy toward China. The United States wanted to erode the Sino-Soviet bloc. China also had a compelling reason to change its policy. Its economic expansion policy needed to have entry into the US market, and it needed to have the ability to work with the World Trade Organization and to attract foreign investment. Although not nearly as dramatically as with China, US-Cuba relations are showing some similarities in favoring change. Normalizing the relationship with Cuba will help the United States improve its relationships in the Western hemisphere.

Other lessons emerge from experiences closer to home. The United States and Cuba both need to aim for mutual respect and abandon jousting, and for any chance of success, the US national interest has to override the parochial Miami Mania opposition.

The United States and Cuba have survived the "un-normal" relationship for more than fifty years. What are the reasons to change that now, and how compelling are they?

Greater US exports to Cuba can help the US economy. Unlike for China and Vietnam, the trade balance will probably favor the United States. Will it greatly change the US economy? No. But it will have a positive economic impact in the Midwest, the Southeast, and the Gulf states. These states could be shipping to Cuba not only agricultural goods but automobiles, machinery, household goods, construction materials, and more; the Gulf region could be a distribution hub for Cuba.

Can the United States and Cuba aim for mutual respect and abandon the tit-for-tat approach? Can a greater US national interest override the parochial interest of the Miami Mania mentality? From the Cuban side, normal relations would greatly boost tourism, improve the country's ability to obtain credit, enhance foreign investment, foster Cuban exports to the United States, and make goods and services available to complement the Cuban government's policy of promoting greater privatization. This normalization will help Cuba vastly improve its economic situation. It will help stop the brain drainage of Cuban youth seeking opportunity elsewhere, and it will help provide the economic resources needed to maintain and upgrade the social programs that are so important to Cuba.

Cuba has more and better reasons to press for normalization than the United States has. While pressing for social changes, the United States can afford to be magnanimous and need not try to be omnipotent. On the other hand, how far will the Cuban government go in liberalizing its political and economic systems?

There is little question that better relations with Cuba would improve US relations in the rest of the Americas. As we see in the public perspectives on China in the Latin American countries, the US national interest would be well served; there is much more at stake than merely facilitating Cuba's readmission to the Organization of American States.

Julia Sweig, a Cuba scholar at the Council on Foreign Relations, put it this way. "Fifty years after the US…made Cuba its litmus test for its commercial and diplomatic ties in Latin America, Latin America is turning the tables."[5] If there is no single, overriding reason to normalize relations with Cuba, there certainly are several good reasons to do so. So what are the obstacles?

A proembargo article from the Cuba Transition Project at the University of Miami serves as a good point of departure to discuss building bridges between the two countries.[6] It makes the case that the Castro brothers are not naïve and will not allow US tourism to subvert the regime, that tourists will not bring democracy to Cuba or lead to economic growth or political change, and that engagement with a totalitarian state will not bring about its demise.

Jay: I think we can agree that the Castro Brothers are not naïve.

Maria: They would not have been around for so long!

Jay: I think we can also agree that American tourists will not bring democracy to Cuba. Leaders would indeed have to be naïve to agree to the subversion or demise of their government. Not only did the leaders of China, Vietnam, and Myanmar not agree to subversive terms in exchange for normalization, but the US government did not request them.

We have to agree that the "good neighbor" should not be interpreted as "I am good, and you are my neighbor." It has taken the United States more than 230 years to evolve to our present political system, and there is no question that we still have much evolving to do.

The real question is whether the United States and Cuba will be better off with normalized relations. Will the two countries benefit politically and economically? I think there is no question that both populations will be better off. China has not become a democracy, but many Chinese citizens have seen substantial improvements in their standards of living because of the trade and tourism between the United States and China.

Maria: The same can be said of Vietnam, which has a large population presence in the United States; these people visit their homeland on a regular basis and are supporting their relatives back home. Some have created joint business partnerships. Why shouldn't we do the same with Cuba?

Jay: Will improvements in the standard of living have an impact on the form of government? Economic growth leads to greater aspirations, which, in turn, have an impact on the form of government. The Cuban government may not evolve into the Miami-Mania model, but freedom of movement and economic growth will impact the Cuban form of government.

A friend of mine in Cuba once asked me why the United States was so afraid to permit US citizens to travel to Cuba. "If the ideas and culture they bring with them are so strong, they will cause a change," he said. With the new travel policy implemented by President Obama, we can now better appraise the impact.

Maria: If that is the case, then we can argue that removing restrictions on travel and trade, so as to bring about one-on-one contact, can help drive change.

Some groups, however, refuse to acknowledge that change is already taking place. A prime example is the current law issued by Raúl Castro allowing Cubans—including some of the so-called dissidents—to travel abroad.

It's important to understand that because of the economic size of the United States and its geographic closeness, demographic composition, cultural history, and political system, its actions in Cuba simply have a much greater impact than, say, tourism and trade from Canada or Spain. The majority of the Cuban population has a tremendous affinity with the American people and everything American. As you walk out of the José Martí airport, you see a huge billboard proclaiming the evils of the embargo. That sign is not about Spanish policy.

Now, expropriation without compensation is not a good policy to follow. It is not good for countries that want to invest in other countries, and it is not good for countries that want to encourage foreign investment.

But we should also remember that expropriation problems are not new. The United States has negotiated these problems with Mexico, the Soviet Union, China, Yugoslavia, Bulgaria, Romania, Hungary, and Poland. Cuba's expropriation of US property was substantial and should not be ignored. Yet historically, the United States has found ways to resolve such problems while maintaining diplomatic relations.

There are creative ways to resolve them, as we saw in the STET-ITT resolution in Cuba.[7] There are civil ways to approach the problem, as we are also seeing in the YPF-Repsol negotiations in Argentina. For the good of the United States and Cuba, the problem should be resolved.[8]

From the Cuban standpoint, there is a great temptation to link the cost of the embargo to negotiations on expropriation. From the US side, the temptation is to link expropriation with the form of government. If the purpose is to get to "yes" on this issue, both sides have to be flexible.

The United States and Cuba are already building bridges. It may come as a surprise to some to know that relations between military units of the two countries are quite civil. Officers from the Guantanamo Naval Base and from the Cuban Armed Forces meet regularly at the naval gate, which is widely known as the "Gate of Talks."

The US Coast Guard and the Cuban Border Guard work together on several issues of mutual interest: drug intervention, migration, and search and rescue involving people in distress at sea. Their relationship has been fruitful and is characterized by mutual respect and cooperation.

Cuba and the National Ocean and Atmospheric Administration (NOAA) have a close working relationship in determining the path of hurricanes. According to Max Mayfield, who retired in 2007 as director of the National Hurricane Center in Miami, "We've had a close working relationship in regard to tropical cyclones that goes back to the '70s. Any storm that goes toward Florida goes over Cuba, so we need their observation, and they need our data from the aircraft."[9]

In 2010 Haiti suffered a devastating earthquake. At the time, more than three hundred Cuban doctors were conducting humanitarian work in the country. US State Department spokesperson Darby Holladay issued this communiqué: "The United States has communicated its readiness to make medical relief supplies available to Cuban doctors working on the ground in Haiti as part of the international relief effort."[10] As a sign of cooperation, Cuba authorized American medical-evacuation flights to go through Cuban airspace, which allowed the US medical-evacuation team to cut ninety minutes off travel time from Haiti to Miami.

On January 12, 2011, US and Cuban representatives met for the fourth time to resume the discussions of the US-Cuba Migration Accords. The US team was led by the Deputy Assistant Secretary of State for Western Hemisphere Affairs, Roberta Jacobson; and the Cuban delegation was led by Vice Minister Dagoberto Rodriguez Barrera. Jacobson reaffirmed the US commitment to promoting safe, legal, and orderly migration.

There is a limited number of nongovernmental organizations working in Cuba. Universities including Harvard, the University of Alabama, the University of Florida, the University of Texas, and the University of Havana have educational exchanges.

On June 24, 2013, lawmakers were informed that the United States and Cuba would resume talks that week aimed at ending a fifty-year suspension of direct-mail service. Cuba and the United States have not had direct service since 1963. The only way mail reaches Cuba is through a third country.

We can also tally numerous lost opportunities. While the rest of the world has relations with Cuba and permits investments in Cuba, the United

States continues its policy of limiting commercial activity. Ironically, the largest and closest US trading partners, Canada and Mexico, are taking far greater advantage of commercial relations with Cuba.

Business relations between the United States and the Dominican Republic give some indication of what trade and investment patterns might look like under normalized relations between the United States and Cuba. Presently, the United States sells about four hundred million dollars of goods annually to Cuba. There are no investments. In 2012, the United States exported $7.3 billion in goods to the Dominican Republic, and in the prior five years, US businesses invested more than five billion dollars there.[11]

In time, Cuba should represent an even greater opportunity for US trade and investment. If substantial amounts of oil are discovered in Cuba, the United States could sell Cuba an estimated additional five billion dollars in goods and services in the petroleum sector.

Cuba too is losing opportunities. It exports practically nothing to the United States. Returning to the Dominican example, in 2012, the Dominican Republic exported $3.1 billion to the United States.

If there were no travel restrictions, Cuba could expect to see an increase in travel for both tourism and business from the present level of around four hundred thousand US travelers to well over one million per year. To the amazement of many, travel and trade with Cuba are already substantial. At the peak of prerevolution tourism in 1957, Cuba attracted 272,265 American tourists. Now, more than four hundred thousand people travel between the United States and Cuba every year. In 2012, the number of Cuban Americans traveling to Cuba was 475,936, and Cuba received 98,050 US citizens who were not Cuban American. Vessels sail for Cuba every week carrying US goods.

The Office of Foreign Assets Control (OFAC) increased the number of charter-flight companies from twelve in 2011 to thirty-one in 2012, making it easier for Cuban Americans and other US citizens to travel to Cuba. The vast majority of the charter companies for US-Cuba travel are operated by Cuban exiles. The number of agencies operating in the United

States that are licensed to sell tickets on Cuba-bound flights rose from 68 agencies in 2011 to 328 agencies in 2012. During a one-month period, travel agencies had estimated revenues of $23,764,500 from ticket sales alone. During a one-month period, there were 230 established flights to several destinations in Cuba. Travelers to Cuba spent an average of $3,500 in cash to cover expenses, which are estimated at a total of $2.2 billion a year. This too is changing with the Obama Administration, as airlines are looking at direct flights to Cuba, and ferry services have been authorized to Cuba. Again, it will be a long process. Cubana de Aviacion, Cuba's airline, will ask for landing rights in the United States in return. With the authorization from OFAC in establishing ferry services, it remains to be seen what guide lines Cuba will esyablish.

Given the scale of these numbers even with the embargo in place, it is clear that lifting the embargo would provide dramatic opportunities for growth, which, in turn, would provide Cuba with better options for engagement with international banking entities such as the World Bank, the International Money Fund, and Inter-American Development Bank.

There are two prime reasons why the United States did not demand that China or Vietnam become instant democracies. First, the United States could not make them become democracies, any more than we can make Cuba do so. It simply was not realistic to assume that China or Vietnam would summarily scrap their forms of government, just as it is unrealistic to expect Cuba to do so. Second, the United States had urgent reasons to normalize relations with both China and Vietnam.

While the embargo is still in place, we continue to have a double standard for Cuba. There are now enough compelling reasons that at least the double standard should disappear. Why do we still have an embargo?

11

After the Euphoria

Jay: I happened to be in Cuba on December 17. After I crossed the tarmac and entered the smaller José Martí terminal used for Miami flights, my first encounter offered a taste of the Cuban response to President Obama's announcement. A Cuban customs official came up to me and gave me a huge hug. "Tomorrow is my fifty-sixth birthday," she said, "and what a great present Obama and Castro have given me!" Her spontaneous welcome, not to mention the open admission of her age, spoke volumes about the impact the announcement had.

In appointment after appointment, there was a complete change in attitude about why we were meeting and what the future held. For the first time since I began to travel to Cuba, we were no longer just talking about when relations would improve; we were talking about the possibilities of cooperation. But there was also a small voice that kept saying, "This all will take time." I recalled Tina Rosenberg's book *The Haunted Land*, an excellent study of the post-Soviet transition in Eastern Europe. She wrote, "Nations, like individuals, need to face up to and understand traumatic events before they can put them aside and move on to a normal life."[1]

Maria: There are a lot of transitions all at once. When the wall came down in Berlin, East and West Germany did not suddenly become one big happy family. Similarly, the conflicts between the United States and Cuba have not suddenly gone away. Miami Mania may take on a new life related to how "they" will change Cuba. As for Cuba, it was already facing a number of challenges, including other shifting, traumatic circumstances:

Fidel Castro stepping down, the faltering of the Venezuelan economic and political structure, and the reality that Cubans can no longer expect cradle-to-grave state care and will have to become more self-reliant.

Let's look at some of the problems that Cuba was facing before December 17, keeping in mind that the date may or may not be a game changer, but it is certainly a mind changer. Aspirations grow; if they are not tempered and met, they can lead to frustration. At this juncture Cuba is faced with managing economic growth and maintaining government stability.

WE NEED TO EXAMINE SOME OF THE CRITICAL FACTORS IN THE TRANSITIONAL PROCESS.

Is there a Castro vacuum syndrome? With Fidel's departure from the public eye, Raúl Castro has implemented his own brand, Raúlismo, a more pragmatic military governing process. Cuba has already commenced this transition, with its ups and downs. Raúl Castro made it clear to lawmakers that he wants better relations with the United States but that Cuba will never give in to US demands for changes in its government and economy. "We do not demand that the US change its political and social system, and we do not expect negotiations over ours."[2]

President Raúl Castro has promised to step down by 2018, at which time his successor will assume power, once elected by *el Consejo de Estado*.[3] Cuba will not change overnight, contrary to the apparent hopes of many in the exile community, and certainly not into a political system patterned after the US model. Because of the formalized transition process, it is fair to assume that there will be no vacuum in the government without the Castros. The transitional process has already started.

With President Raúl Castro's departure from government, a new generation will take power. What will be the role of the Communist Party? Will Cuba develop a communist system like China or Vietnam? Will it evolve like Eastern Europe or like the other former Soviet countries, where the business tycoons of today are often the same people formerly in power? Cuba will most likely remain a one-party state; its party is similar to the historical role of the PRI in Mexico, with the central government as the country's economic planner.

We must not forget the military influence in governing. Any changes will be directly tied to the economic conditions Cuba faces at the time. The military will act as technocrats and will participate in the decision-making process in conjunction with the Communist Party.

Cuba's economic reforms are directly tied to the island's current economic situation. If the Cuban economy improves, the economic changes will be slower. On the other hand, an economic crisis in Cuba will accelerate economic measures. Cuba has highly beneficial trade agreements with Venezuela, providing much-needed petroleum, technical assistance, and financial investment. If the political situation in Venezuela changes, it could be catastrophic to Cuba's economy.

Venezuela's future is still to be determined, and for Cuba the outcome is crucially important. Cuba gets about one hundred thousand barrels of oil a day from Venezuela at a price of around eight dollars a barrel. It uses some of the oil and sells the rest at a substantial profit. President Maduro in April announced that Venezuela was cutting its oil supply to Cuba in half, which will not only affect Cuba but all the Petrocaribe countries. In addition, about eighteen thousand Cubans live in Venezuela, a large number of them doctors—for whom Cuba is paid. Cuba also has a presence in Venezuela's army and secret police. The fact that a special building has been designated to serve Cubans at Maiquetia International Airport (serving Caracas) gives an idea of the magnitude of the ties. If the Cuba-friendly regime falls in Venezuela, Cuba is in trouble. It does not have a good plan *B*.

Political analyst Roger Noriega, who was a State Department official in the George W. Bush Administration, considers the regime of this Cuban neighbor to be on its last legs. "Venezuelan President Nicolás Maduro is fighting a losing battle to salvage his regime…As details of his government's bankruptcy are made public, his political base will continue to splinter. And as he follows Cuban advice to use brute force against peaceful demonstrators, the nationalist military will find the growing violence intolerable. In short, Maduro's condition is terminal."[4]

Venezuela's international reserves are too low, and "what is left in the bank would cover the cost of about two weeks' worth of imports. So shortages of essential goods will worsen in the days ahead," Noriega gauged. Venezuela is not keeping up with oil deliveries, and Noriega calls oil production faltering and oversubscribed. He says Hugo Chávez commanded the respect or fear of uniformed services, but Maduro has earned little respect within their ranks.

A nationalist wing chafes at the heavy-handed role of the Cuban regime in Maduro's administration. As one former Chávez confidant grumbled privately, "There is not a *chavista* government in Venezuela today—it is a Cuban government instead. The images of ill-trained national guardsmen and civilian thugs shooting, beating, and detaining student protesters have further alienated the bulk of the army officer corps from Maduro and his cadre of corrupt generals."

Keep in mind that Cuba has some skills in the arena of surviving economic implosions, given what was learned during the "Special Period" following the collapse of the USSR. Still, we must wonder whether people in Cuba are ready to face another economic crisis like the one they endured in the 1990s. Some of the reforms President Raúl Castro is undertaking are designed to help see Cuba through in case of another *Período Especial*, and for safety's sake, he is cultivating closer economic ties with Brazil, Russia, China, and Iran.

Change is not easy. To some degree, Cuba's objectives are in direct internal conflict. For example, looking at some of the current changes in Cuba, such as the large segment of revenue derived from exports of medical services, remittances from Cuban exiles, and earnings in the tourist sector, it is clear that all these activities greatly impact the population, creating unintended consequences. Exports of medical services, for example, indirectly degrade Cuba's quality of medical care for its own people, provoking resentment from the population. The fact that remittance recipients achieve a higher standard of living than the rest of the population causes internal tensions, less dependency on the government, and the emergence of a new social class.

We should note that people whom the government lai
mitted to start their own businesses, resulting in their bec
pendent on the current system. The irony is that this runs   .. .o key
principles of the Cuban Revolution. In reality, the remittances and small
businesses hinder the government's influence on the political structure and
diminish its control over people. Some of the businesses already existed in
the black market, and in that sense, we can see that the government is obtaining more economic control and added income through licensing and
taxation, while at the same time yielding economic power, influence, and
control.

Cuba wants to reactivate economic growth while retaining the political
structure and social benefits. Encouraging private economic growth, much
of it financed by the Cuban exile community, will sooner or later challenge
the political and economic model. Members of the exile community with
family on the island are indirectly financing many business enterprises.

Some members of the exile community are already participating in
joint ventures with family members to establish small businesses. For example, a Cuban exile can indirectly purchase several cars and lease them
to others on the island for the purpose of operating a nongovernment taxi
service. *Paladares*, small privately operated restaurants, are also being financed by families in exile.

Cuba will control the large corporate investments by establishing pre-
conditions for incentives, work force, taxes, property leases, and repatria-
tion of profits. Even if changes take place in US policy, companies need
to educate and inform themselves about Cuba's new investment laws.
An example is the special zone near the Port of Mariel. "The laws grant
tax benefits starting November 2013 to companies working in the economic zone around the port, about 465 square kilometers." Among them
are tax exemptions on their labor force and on profits for a ten-year period. Companies operating in the area do not have to pay taxes on sales
or services for the first twelve months of operations. Also planned is the
duty-free entry of "means, equipment, and goods imported for purposes of
investment in the area."[5]

One of Cuba's biggest problems is migration of the young population. The government has invested a tremendous amount of capital in educating the next generation, and a large proportion of the beneficiaries are migrating for economic reasons. There is a mass exodus, and Cuba has an aging population that needs to be replaced in order to contribute to the future of the country. Like all young people, young Cubans want purchasing power and the ability to live independently. They want to travel and have a vision for their futures. The government of Cuba needs to address the problem of their departure and develop a viable solution.

The United States has matters to address too. The US government spends a lot of resources via the Department of State, Department of Commerce, and the US Treasury's Office of Foreign Assets Control (OFAC) to enforce a policy that has not achieved its intended purpose. At least ten government agencies are responsible for enforcing different provisions of the embargo. According to the Government Accountability Office, hundreds of millions of dollars and tens of thousands of work hours are applied to enforcing the embargo; most people would probably view all this as pouring money down a rat hole every year for fifty years.[6]

It is extremely important to understand that President Obama's initiative did not end the embargo. US policy on the Cuban embargo remains in place and causes conflict within the Americas, starting with Canada. The big challenge now is to obtain the cooperation of Congress to repeal the various laws that govern the embargo.

The December 17 change in US policy has, nevertheless, sent a strong message, and an end to the Cuban embargo would send a powerful message to all of Latin America that the United States wants a warmer and stronger relationship with its neighbors to the south. Given current shifts in US, Cuban, and Venezuelan policies, now is an opportune moment to move forward with legislative changes.

Benefits for the United States go far beyond looking less like a bully. Besides improving relations in the Americas, fuller trade and investment relations would ensue, as outlined in the preceding chapter in the summary of US-Dominican trade and investment.

The US Chamber of Commerce estimates that the Cuban embargo costs the United States $1.2 billion annually in exports, and the figure could be much higher. Normalized relations between the two countries would also permit cooperation for better environmental protection of the waters and shores of both countries.

Benefits for Cuba start with capital for investment. If the small-business sector is to grow, it needs capital. One source is the Cuban exile community. In effect, normalized relations would legitimize what is already taking place. Cuba also needs substantially greater investments in its infrastructure to attract and keep a high level of tourism, and it needs to have the ability to use the international organizations such as the International Money Fund, World Bank, and World Trade Organization. The Cuban government estimates that there is a need for an annual inflow of between 2.5 and 4 billion dollars.

If the huge investment in Mariel is to pay off, Cuba needs the ability to attract transshipment vessels and develop the industrial zone at Mariel. The industrial trade zones would be complementary for Florida and the Gulf states. A greater export market is essential. Even if oil is found in substantial quantities, Cuba needs to broaden its economy while having political stability.

Stepping back for a moment, consider the Central American country of Honduras. It is a wonderful country with some of the nicest people you would ever want to meet. It is a country that now has the third largest *maquiladora* (apparel assembly) sector in the world. In addition to its traditional crops of coffee and bananas, Honduras has developed a large export market for shrimp as well as hugely growing exports in nontraditional fruits and vegetables. Puerto Cortes has experienced large investments and growth, and the free-trade zones are flourishing. There are parallels here with Cuba's investment in Mariel and the opening of the Industry Development Zone. But there is another side to Honduras. It is the second poorest country in Central America, and it is one of the most dangerous countries in the world. According to an article by Philip Sherwell, the murder rate was eighty-five for every hundred thousand residents in

2012.[7] There is an epidemic of gang and drug violence, and drug gangs threaten the viability of the Honduran state. The huge flow of children from Honduras to the United States in 2014 underlines these continuing problems.

The point is that a country is built on a fragile "ecosystem." The opening of opportunity for small businesses is good, the spread of the *paladares* (small family-run eateries) is constructive, the attracting of properly controlled foreign investments is necessary, and improvements in human rights are imperative, but a stable political system is essential. Is it desirable to have a sudden "Cuban Spring"? With the new breath of fresh air ushered in by the actions of President Obama and President Castro, would it not be better to permit Cuba all four seasons in developing a better economic and political system for its people? External pressures from the US government added to the influence of Miami Mania plus internal pressures in Cuba could push too hard.

The December 17 White House announcement outlines the facilitation of financial transactions between the United States and Cuba. The US trade embargo is still in place and prohibits direct US investment. However, in removing Cuba from the list of state sponsors of terrorism, there are important restricted issues that need to be reviewed.

1. The US administration should concentrate on dealing with international financial institutions such as the International Monetary Fund, the World Bank, and the Inter-American Development Bank and trade.

    US policy should take into consideration that the BRICS (Brazil, Russia, India, China, South Africa) grouping's New Development Bank (NDB) is now a reality. While NDB may have greater concentration in the Asian area, four of the founding members—Brazil, Russia, China, and South Africa—are long-time Cuban allies. (Not to ignore India, but historically, it has been less active in Cuba.)

The development of the Mariel port and Industrial Development Zone are already heavily influenced by Brazil and China. While the US Embargo does not permit direct US investment, there is now the possibility of opening a "window" of financial intention by encouraging the use of traditional international financial institutions and the Generalized System of Preferences.

2. Drop the provisions of the embargo. (The executive can do much to normalize relations even while Congress debates legislative changes.) The president's December 17 announcement has done much to remove certain restrictions of the embargo. Both OFAC and the Department of Commerce are working on new provisions and will continue to explore avenues that can be opened—subject to negotiations in the United States and Cuba. While this process is going on, the laws that codify the embargo are still in place. Congressional procedures are not built to promote rapid change. As we have shown, a relatively small number of legislators can do a great deal to stop change. The administration needs to be clear on what needs to be done and reach out for support to make it happen.

3. Close Radio y Televisión Martí and save the taxpayers money wasted on government-funded broadcasting.

4. Change US immigration policy to abandon the "wet foot/dry foot" distinction.

5. Seek creative ways to settle the question of expropriated property.

Cuba could:

1. Try to avoid the tit-for-tat system of negotiation. Trading concessions are understandable; sometimes it is more blessed to give than to receive.

2. Clearly outline how foreign investment can be made in Cuba: rules, restrictions, and protection. With the new investment law for Mariel, the government needs to clarify questions on how foreign investments can be made. It could set up an office in Washington

to deal specifically with parties interested in doing business in Cuba to direct people to appropriate contacts, provide information requested, and facilitate meetings and negotiations.

3. Recognize change in immigration policy.
4. Underline the Cuban government's interest in working on the control of narcotraffic.
5. Seek creative ways to settle the question of expropriated property.
6. Build better bridges with the Cuban American community.
7. Realistically approach the effort to claim for the cost of the embargo.
8. The Cuban government has clearly stated that it requires $2.2 billion dollars of foreign investment in the next five years to achieve the economic transformation in the Cuban economic model. International financing will play a significant role in this process.

The business sector, ordinary citizens, academia, and government officials can also take a more active role in promoting relations.

1. They can become familiar with US-Cuban relations and take the time to educate themselves.
2. Businesses that have products they would like to export to Cuba or import from Cuba can find out if they are in compliance and obtain the appropriate licenses.
3. Contact senators and representatives and discuss their feelings about improving relations with Cuba.
4. State and local governments can look at what their region could be selling to Cuba and the potential economic impact.
5. Academia can encourage academic exchanges and make US-Cuban relations a study project, without taking sides, so that students learn how policy is made and how countries interact; there is a tremendous amount to be learned.
6. National representatives should represent their country fairly but can also speak frankly with leaders to encourage them to improve

relations between the two countries, especially now that Cuba is in a transitional period. They can encourage that transition; constructive actions will lead to positive reactions.

7. US representatives and senators can look at repealing the laws that prohibit better relations and that thereby hinder economic growth for their states.

8. All parties can focus on constructing personal relationships to facilitate the possibility of joint business ventures.

Maria: Let's not forget the harm that this policy has done to the United States—its moral and political impact. "Plausible deniability" was a central tenet for the Kennedy Administration in developing its policy toward Cuba. When the United States becomes obsessed with assassinating a leader, that is a problem. Talking works much better.

Jay: What are our main conclusions and messages? Cool heads and foresight can take a project some of the way, but handling political intricacies also requires transparency and mutually respectful exchange, even when people disagree. Maria Conchita and I are only a microcosm, but we have seen and shown that two diverse philosophies can "conspire" effectively.

Maria: We are proud of our respective roles in the world of marine transportation and of how we have helped facilitate trade relations between the United States and Cuba. Over and over again, we have seen how the actions of *individuals* can make a difference. That's why we outline the seven steps business people can take, beyond the steps that governments can take. In the words attributed to anthropologist Margaret Mead, "Never doubt that a small group of thoughtful, committed citizens can change the world. Indeed, it's the only thing that ever has."

Jay: As we have seen, US-Cuba foreign policy has been taken over by a small group, in this case the Cuban Americans at the center of what we call Miami Mania. Most people in the United States don't have a clear idea of how foreign policy is often made. It has been difficult to explain this to Cuban government officials and to the average Cuban or American person on the street.

As an example, before the December 17 announcement, one of the questions I was most often asked in Cuba was, "When is the United States government going to change its policy toward Cuba?" I, in turn, would ask questioners if they understood the role of the Cuban American community in not having that policy changed. Most did not. December 17 is only the beginning. Laws still need to be changed and a small group of legislators can either facilitate or hinder those changes. If there were maybe twenty Maria Conchitas, the United States would have a different policy.

President Obama was clear in stating that the present policies of both countries are failing to serve their own best interests. We are neighbors; it's time to be good neighbors. The majority of the population in both countries is in favor of better relations. The people now need to support their leaders' decisions to improve relations.

Maria: There is nothing easy about being a leader. We have to applaud President Obama and President Castro for setting changes in motion.

Jay: On January 26, 2014, as we flew from Miami to Cuba, I talked with Mr. Bautise, St. Lucia's minister of trade and development. I asked him if normalizing US relations with Cuba would be good for St. Lucia. He said normalization would probably not be good for St. Lucia, because it would draw tourism away from his nation. But he added that he nevertheless favored such a change, because US policy toward Cuba made the United States look hypocritical in promoting good relations in the Americas. "US policy toward Cuba," he said, "is like a wound in the heart of the Americas."

On the US side, the question I hear most often is, "When are the Cubans going to let us in?" I know only one way to reply: "When the United States lifts the embargo." The time has come.

12

No Excuses, *Basta Ya*

On January 27, 2014, Cuban President Raúl Castro and Brazilian President Dilma Rousseff officially opened Cuba's new port and container terminal at Mariel forty miles west of Havana, a complex that cost $957 million. Cuba's largest infrastructure project in decades, the new port was built by a Brazilian construction company with financing from a Brazilian development bank, and it will be managed by PSA International of Singapore.

The Mariel Industrial Development Zone is contiguous to the port. In combination, this facility and the mega port are "aimed in particular at providing a stopover for vessels transiting through the Panama Canal, and to accommodate extra consignments in anticipation that the United States' embargo will be eventually be lifted," noted the news service Tax-News.com. "Brazil is proud to partner with Cuba in this historical container port in the Caribbean," said Brazilian president Rousseff.[1]

Jay: What the article did not say is that the Industrial Development Zone will be the real driving factor in the growth of the port—and US-Cuba trade relations have to be in place to bring the project to its full potential. As I stood on the dock watching the breeze flutter the flags on the Crowley vessel, the irony of what was happening was not lost. The first vessel to deliver cargo to this port was a Crowley vessel that had sailed from Port Everglades, Florida.[2] These types of coincidences do not happen in Cuba. No subtlety here. Trade from the United States was welcomed.

Also attending the port inauguration ceremony were several other heads of state: Presidents Evo Morales of Bolivia, Nicolás Maduro of Venezuela, Michel Martelly of Haiti, Donald Ramotar of Guyana, and Portia Simpson-Miller, Prime Minister of Jamaica. They were all in Havana that week for the second summit of the Community of Latin American and Caribbean States. "Only with Cuba [aboard] will our region be complete," declared Rousseff during the CELAC meeting.[3]

As always, when it comes to Cuba, ironies reign, in this case, several of them swirling around a single port. Mariel used to be a US Navy base. The 1980 boatlift that brought 125,000 Cuban refugees to the United States came from Mariel. Cuba has financed and built its Mariel mega port without any US participation, yet the first vessel into Mariel was from the very country that is embargoing Cuba.

For this port and industrial zone to be a success, Cuba needs trade with the United States.

Other stars were aligning in the Florida Straits. On January 28, 2014, the day after the Port of Mariel opening, President Obama delivered his State of the Union address. "I am eager to work with all of you," the president told Congress. "But America does not stand still, and neither will I. So whenever I can take steps without legislation to expand opportunity for more American families, that's what I'm going to do."[4] Cuban Americans were conscious of one more irony. January 28 was the birthday of Cuban independence hero José Martí, 161 years before. President Obama was saying he had executive powers available to him—would he use them in relation to Cuba?

Maria: Relations between the United States and Cuba have long been fraught. There is no going back to where we once were. For those who want Cuba to be as they remember it, there is nowhere much to go at all. Gertrude Stein wrote the cruelest analysis of nostalgia. Returning after an absence of thirty-five years to Oakland, the town of her childhood, she found once she got there that "there is no there there."[5] Most of us come from immigrant families; our forebears came to the United States because things were not good where they were, and they wanted to build a better life. And most of us relish, rather than resent, the connection to some prior family homeland—we do not waste energy punishing its current inhabitants.

Normalization will take away the excuse of the embargo for all that is not right in Cuba. If the United States is no longer the enemy, Cuba can relinquish its siege mentality and move ahead on economic and political reforms, and 11.2 million people in Cuba can benefit in ways that many of their families have done in the United States.

Normalization requires and entails mutual respect, diplomatic relations, commercial trade, free flow of travel, and each country staying out of the domestic politics and economic development of the other. The United States needs to move away from the mentality that we will "help" Cuba. Let's help Detroit; let's help New Orleans; and let's ease up and allow Cuba to move ahead. Cuba has to decide how to plan its own future.

Cuba does need to make some changes. The Cuban approach has basically been that US policies were made arbitrarily, it is up to the United States to change those policies, and Cuba should not be expected to make any changes. But as noted in the previous chapter, there are several ways in which Cuba can make changes that would improve relations with the United States.

Jay: We need to recognize that, even now, US policy toward Cuba in effect remains stuck on its two original objectives: to overthrow the Castro government and prevent the Cuban sociopolitical model from spreading to other parts of the Caribbean and Central and South America.

The Cuban model has not taken over the Western Hemisphere. Democracy has been growing apace in most of the Americas. The Castro government is still there, but even it now recognizes that the model needs to change.

In order to move ahead following the December 17 announcement aimed at resuming diplomatic relations, it is important to keep some things in mind.

First, December 17 is only the beginning. The meetings in Panama between President Obama and President Raúl Castro are just stepping stones to a long road. Inertia can return; momentum can be lost in the heat of prolonged negotiations. Both countries face a number of economic and political problems that could distract from the final goal of normal relations.

Second, we must keep in mind that there is no good reason for the embargo. After World War II, the United States had pressing reasons to normalize relations even with our bitterest enemies. During the Cold War, we found ways to normalize relations with China and later with Vietnam and Myanmar. There is no good reason not to continue to implement and expand on the December 17 announcement. President Obama said, "The Cold War is over."

There are both good and worthy reasons to do so. Cuba and the United States are neighbors. After Canada and Mexico, Cuba is our closest neighbor. We are Cuba's closest neighbor. The development of the two countries is historically interwoven. The cultural ties are tremendous. The economies are complementary. Normalized relations would benefit both countries.

Our two countries have a history that both unites us and divides us. To put matters in perspective, if we were to rate the level of conflict between the two countries on a scale of one to ten, with ten being an enemy in a world war, the relationship might qualify as a three or four.

Third, not talking to each other formally for more than fifty years certainly makes meaningful conversation awkward, and various US laws are obstacles for negotiations; there may even be constitutional questions about some of the restrictions. The executive branch has a great deal of latitude to negotiate these items, but the underlying laws need to be repealed.

Fourth, two of the most important laws that should be repealed are the Cuban Democracy Act of 1992 and the Cuban Liberty and Democratic Solidarity Act of 1996 (Helms-Burton).

Fifth, if both countries want to normalize relations, it is time to put history aside, embrace mutual respect, and show greater flexibility. As Margaret MacMillan observed of World War I, "In the end, the decisions that took Europe into that war—or failed to prevent it—were made by a surprisingly small number."[6] The decision to normalize relations between the United States and Cuba is likewise a decision that lies with a tiny group of people in each country, although the positive impact will be felt by millions.

The Cuban government has signaled its willingness to tango. Close to half a million Cuban Americans are already traveling to Cuba each year. US ships are already routinely calling at Havana and Mariel. What it comes down to now is that when enough players are ready to abandon Miami Mania in favor of broader goals, the embargo will go away.

People in the United States can make a difference. Whether in South Florida or elsewhere, we can nudge our representatives to understand that there is no political capital in supporting the present US-Cuba policy. And some particular individuals can provoke changes of direction more readily than most of us can.

Less than a week after the grand opening of the Port of Mariel and President Obama's State of the Union address, prominent Cuban businessman Alfonso Fanjul was quoted in the *Washington Post* on February 2, 2014, saying he would "look at" investing in Cuba "if there's an arrangement within Cuba and the United States, and legally it can be done, and there's a proper framework set up and in place."[7]

Fanjul left Cuba as a young man, his family abandoning their mansion and vast sugarcane fields as the Castro regime began its expropriations. Now in his seventies, Fanjul has built an even larger sugar empire during his exile in the United States. Among the family holdings today are Domino Sugar and refineries in the United States, Europe, and Latin America.

He has begun to revisit the island and "tentatively eye Cuba as a place for him and other US businessmen to expand their enterprises." His remarks to the *Post* were cautious, circumspect, and general, but his message was clear. The reporting team noted, "Fanjul's about-face is a startling development for the exile network that has held a grip on the politics of US-Cuba relations for decades and has played an outsized role in presidential campaigns. His trips place him at the vanguard of a group of ultrawealthy

US investors with roots on the island whose economic interests and political clout are pushing the two countries toward a thaw in their half-century standoff."[8]

"Keep in mind," said Fanjul, "that when Castro came to power, I was a young man. So the notion that the same policies that we put in place in 1961 would somehow still be as effective…today in the age of the Internet and Google and world travel doesn't make sense."

Cuban American businessman Paul Cejas has likewise expressed doubts about the embargo. A former US ambassador to Belgium, he too has traveled to Cuba. He is quoted in the *Post* noting, "I can tell you one thing that became very clear to me: the embargo is really an embargo against America ourselves. Because Americans cannot do business with Cuba, where there are incredible opportunities for growth."[9]

We need to ask if, in the case of US-Cuba relations, is parochial interest hindering the greater good? It is growing ever clearer that US policy could be far more dynamic if we did not have to constantly expend diplomatic currency explaining our Cuba policy, as at Organization of American States (OAS) meetings.

Alfonso Fanjul told the *Post* that traveling to the island gave him insights of all kinds. "When you talk with people and hear them, it humanizes. Talking is the first step."[10]

Interviewed for the same article, Miami business executive Carlos Saladrigas echoed that view. He said he had been branded a traitor for wanting to change US policy toward Cuba. We consider it wiser to give Saladrigas the last word. "Do Cuban Americans want to be left out of the picture?" he asked. "You can influence Cuba's future much more by participating in Cuba's future than by staying away."

Appendix 1. Excerpts from History Will Absolve Me, 1953

(from Fidel Castro's speech *La historia me absolverá*, his defense in a 1953 trial for rebellion against the Batista regime; available in English at http://www.marxists.org/history/cuba/archive/castro/1953/10/16.htm)

Are they that afraid of the truth?

Honorable Judges: Why such interest in silencing me? Why is every type of argument foregone in order to avoid presenting any target whatsoever against which I might direct my own brief? Is it that they lack any legal, moral, or political basis on which to put forth a serious formulation of the question? Are they that afraid of the truth? Do they hope that I, too, will speak for only two minutes and that I will not touch upon the points which have caused certain people sleepless nights since July 26th? Since the prosecutor's petition was restricted to the mere reading of five lines of an article of the Social Defense Code, might they suppose that I too would limit myself to those same lines and circle round them like some slave turning a millstone? I shall by no means accept such a gag, for in this trial there is much more than the freedom of a single individual at stake.

Fundamental matters of principle are being debated here, the right of men to be free is on trial, the very foundations of our existence as a civilized and democratic nation are in the balance. When this trial is over, I do not want to have to reproach myself for any principle left undefended, for any truth left unsaid, for any crime not denounced.

An uprising against a usurper of the people's power can never be a crime.

It is a fundamental principle of criminal law that an imputed offense must correspond exactly to the type of crime described by law. If no law applies exactly to the point in question, then there is no offense.

The article in question reads textually, "A penalty of imprisonment of from three to ten years shall be imposed upon the perpetrator of any act aimed at bringing about an armed uprising against the Constitutional Powers of the State. The penalty shall be imprisonment for from five to twenty years in the event that insurrection actually be carried into effect."

In what country is the Honorable Prosecutor living? Who has told him that we have sought to bring about an uprising against the Constitutional Powers of the State? Two things are self-evident. First of all, the dictatorship that oppresses the nation is not a constitutional power, but an unconstitutional one: it was established against the Constitution, over the head of the Constitution, violating the legitimate Constitution of the Republic. The legitimate Constitution is that which emanates directly from a sovereign people. I shall demonstrate this point fully later on, notwithstanding all the subterfuges contrived by cowards and traitors to justify the unjustifiable. Secondly, the article refers to Powers, in the plural, as in the case of a republic governed by a Legislative Power, an Executive Power, and a Judicial Power, which balance and counterbalance one another. We have fomented a rebellion against one single power, an illegal one, which has usurped and merged into a single whole both the Legislative and Executive Powers of the nation, and so has destroyed the entire system that was specifically safeguarded by the Code now under our analysis.

My voice will not be stifled.

I warn you, I am just beginning! If there is in your hearts a vestige of love for your country, love for humanity, love for justice, listen carefully. I know that I will be silenced for many years; I know that the regime will try to suppress the truth by all possible means; I know that there will be a conspiracy to bury me in oblivion. But my voice will not be stifled—it will rise from my breast even when I feel most alone, and my heart will give it all the fire that callous cowards deny it.

Humanity in struggle: Addressing/converting the armed forces

Everyone had instructions, first of all, to be humane in the struggle...

Let me mention two important facts that facilitate an objective judgment of our attitude. First: we could have taken over the regiment simply by seizing all the high-ranking officers in their homes. This possibility was rejected for the very humane reason that we wished to avoid scenes of tragedy and struggle in the presence of their families. Second, we decided not to take any radio station over until the army camp was in our power. This attitude, unusually magnanimous and considerate, spared the citizens a great deal of bloodshed. With only ten men, I could have seized a radio station and called the people to revolt. There is no questioning the people's will to fight.

The regime has emphatically repeated that our Movement did not have popular support. I have never heard an assertion so naïve, and at the same time, so full of bad faith. The regime seeks to show submission and cowardice on the part of the people. They all but claim that the people support the dictatorship; they do not know how offensive this is to the brave Orientales. Santiago thought our attack was only a local disturbance between two factions of soldiers; not until many hours later did they realize what had really happened. Who can doubt the valor, civic pride, and limitless courage of the rebel and patriotic people of Santiago de Cuba? If Moncada had fallen into our hands, even the women of Santiago de Cuba would have risen in arms. Many were the rifles loaded for our fighters by the nurses at the Civilian Hospital. They fought alongside us. That is something we will never forget.

It was never our intention to engage the soldiers of the regiment in combat. We wanted to seize control of them and their weapons in a surprise attack, arouse the people and call the soldiers to abandon the odious flag of the tyranny and to embrace the banner of freedom; to defend the supreme interests of the nation and not the petty interests of a small clique; to turn their guns around and fire on the people's enemies and not on the people, among whom are their own sons and fathers; to unite with the people as the brothers that they are instead of opposing the people as the enemies the government tries to make of them; to march behind the only beautiful ideal worthy of sacrificing one's life—the greatness and happiness of one's country. To those who doubt that many soldiers would have followed us, I ask: What Cuban does not cherish glory? What heart is not set aflame by the promise of freedom?

…As to the rest of the national armed forces, would they have fought against a people in revolt? I declare that they would not! A soldier is made of flesh and blood; he thinks, observes, feels. He is susceptible to the opinions, beliefs, sympathies, and antipathies of the people. If you ask his opinion, he may tell you he cannot express it, but that does not mean he has no opinion. He is affected by exactly the same problems that affect other citizens—subsistence, rent, the education of his children, their future, etc. Everything of this kind is an inevitable point of contact between him and the people and everything of this kind relates him to the present and future situation of the society in which he lives. It is foolish to imagine that the salary a soldier receives from the State—a modest enough salary at that—should resolve the vital problems imposed on him by his needs, duties and feelings as a member of his community.

...I have a right to express an opinion about the armed forces because I defended them when everyone else was silent. And I did this neither as a conspirator, nor from any kind of personal interest—for we then enjoyed full constitutional prerogatives. I was prompted only by humane instincts and civic duty. In those days, the newspaper Alerta *was one of the most widely read because of its position on national political matters. In its pages, I campaigned against the forced labor to which the soldiers were subjected on the private estates of high civil personages and military officers. On March 3, 1952, I supplied the courts with data, photographs, films, and other proof denouncing this state of affairs. I also pointed out in those articles that it was elementary decency to increase army salaries. I should like to know who else raised his voice on that occasion to protest against all this injustice done to the soldiers. Certainly not Batista and company, living well-protected on their luxurious estates, surrounded by all kinds of security measures, while I ran a thousand risks with neither bodyguards nor arms.*

...I want to be just above all else, so I can't blame all the soldiers for the shameful crimes that stain a few evil and treacherous army men. But every honorable and upstanding soldier who loves his career and his uniform is duty-bound to demand and to fight for the cleansing of this guilt, to avenge this betrayal and to see the guilty punished. Otherwise the soldier's uniform will forever be a mark of infamy instead of a source of pride.

...On the other hand, the soldiers endure a worse tyranny than the civilians. They are under constant surveillance, and not one of them enjoys the slightest security in his job. Any unjustified suspicion, any gossip, any intrigue, or denunciation, is sufficient to bring transfer, dishonorable discharge, or imprisonment. Did not Tabernilla, in a memorandum, forbid them to talk with anyone opposed to the government, that is to say, with 99 percent of the people?...What a lack of confidence!...Not even the vestal virgins of Rome had to abide

by such a rule! As for the much publicized little houses for enlisted men, there aren't three hundred on the whole island; yet with what has been spent on tanks, guns, and other weaponry, every soldier might have a place to live. Batista isn't concerned with taking care of the army, but that the army takes care of him! He increases the army's power of oppression and killing but does not improve living conditions for the soldiers. Triple-guard duty, constant confinement to barracks, continuous anxiety, the enmity of the people, uncertainty about the future—this is what has been given to the soldier. In other words, "Die for the regime, soldier, give it your sweat and blood. We shall dedicate a speech to you and award you a posthumous promotion (when it no longer matters) and afterward...we shall go on living luxuriously, making ourselves rich. Kill, abuse, oppress the people. When the people get tired and all this comes to an end, you can pay for our crimes while we go abroad and live like kings. And if one day we return, don't you or your children knock on the doors of our mansions, for we shall be millionaires, and millionaires do not mingle with the poor. Kill, soldier, oppress the people, die for the regime, give your sweat and blood."

No weaponry can vanquish the people.

They have tried to establish the myth that modern arms render the people helpless in overthrowing tyrants. Military parades and the pompous display of machines of war are used to perpetuate this myth and to create a complex of absolute impotence in the people. But no weaponry, no violence can vanquish the people once they are determined to win back their rights.

...This is how people fight when they want to win their freedom; they throw stones at airplanes and overturn tanks!

What does the struggle of the people really mean? Which people? What kind of struggle?

When we speak of struggle and we mention the people, we mean the vast unredeemed masses, those to whom everyone makes promises and who are deceived by all; we mean the people who yearn for a better, more dignified, and more just nation; who are moved by ancestral aspirations to justice, for they have suffered injustice and mockery generation after generation; those who long for great and wise changes in all aspects of their life; people who, to attain those changes, are ready to give even the very last breath they have when they believe in something or in someone, especially when they believe in themselves. The first condition of sincerity and good faith in any endeavor is to do precisely what nobody else ever does, that is, to speak with absolute clarity, without fear. The demagogues and professional politicians who manage to perform the miracle of being right about everything and of pleasing everyone are, necessarily, deceiving everyone about everything. The revolutionaries must proclaim their ideas courageously, define their principles, and express their intentions so that no one is deceived, neither friend nor foe.

In terms of struggle, when we talk about people, we're talking about the six hundred thousand Cubans without work, who want to earn their daily bread honestly without having to emigrate from their homeland in search of a livelihood; the five hundred thousand farm laborers who live in miserable shacks, who work four months of the year and starve the rest, sharing their misery with their children, who don't have an inch of land to till and whose existence would move any heart not made of stone; the four hundred thousand industrial workers and laborers whose retirement funds have been embezzled, whose benefits are being taken away, whose homes are wretched quarters, whose salaries pass from the hands of the boss to those of the moneylender, whose future is a pay reduction and dismissal, whose life is endless work and whose only rest is the tomb; the one hundred thousand small farmers who live and die working land that is not theirs, looking at it with the sadness of Moses gazing at the promised land, to die without ever owning it, who, like feudal serfs, have to pay for the use of their parcel of land by giving up a portion of its produce, who cannot love it, improve it, beautify it, nor plant a cedar or an orange tree on it because they never know when a sheriff will come with the rural guard to evict them from it; the thirty thousand teachers and professors who are so devoted, dedicated, and so necessary to the better destiny of future generations and who are so badly treated and paid; the twenty thousand small businessmen weighed down by debts, ruined by the crisis and harangued by a plague of grafting and venal officials; the ten thousand young professional people: doctors, engineers, lawyers, veterinarians, school teachers, dentists, pharmacists, newspapermen, painters, sculptors, etc., who finish school with their degrees, anxious to work and full of hope, only to find themselves at a dead end, all doors closed to them, and where no ears hear their clamor or supplication. These are the people, the ones who know misfortune and therefore are capable of fighting with limitless courage! To these people whose desperate roads through life have been paved with the bricks of betrayal and false promises, we were not going to say: "We will give you..." but rather: "Here it is, now fight for it with everything you have, so that liberty and happiness may be yours!"

The Five Revolutionary Laws

The five revolutionary laws that would have been proclaimed immediately after the capture of the Moncada Barracks and would have been broadcast to the nation by radio must be included in the indictment.

...The first revolutionary law would have returned power to the people and proclaimed the 1940 Constitution the Supreme Law of the State until such time as the people should decide to modify or change it. And in order to effect its implementation and punish those who violated it— there being no electoral organization to carry this out—the revolutionary movement, as the circumstantial incarnation of this sovereignty, the only source of legitimate power, would have assumed all the faculties inherent therein, except that of modifying the Constitution itself: in other words, it would have assumed the legislative, executive and judicial powers.

...The second revolutionary law would give nonmortgageable and nontransferable ownership of the land to all tenant and subtenant farmers, lessees, share croppers, and squatters who hold parcels of five caballerías *of land or less, and the State would indemnify the former owners on the basis of the rental which they would have received for these parcels over a period of ten years.*

The third revolutionary law would have granted workers and employees the right to share 30 percent of the profits of all the large industrial, mercantile, and mining enterprises, including the sugar mills. The strictly agricultural enterprises would be exempt in consideration of other agrarian laws which would be put into effect.

The fourth revolutionary law would have granted all sugar planters the right to share 55 percent of sugar production and a minimum quota of forty thousand arrobas for all small tenant farmers who have been established for three years or more.

The fifth revolutionary law would have ordered the confiscation of all holdings and ill-gotten gains of those who had committed frauds during previous regimes, as well as the holdings and ill-gotten gains of all their legates and heirs.

...Furthermore, it was declared that the Cuban policy in the Americas would be one of close solidarity with the democratic peoples of this continent, and that all those politically persecuted by bloody tyrannies oppressing our sister nations would find generous asylum, brotherhood, and bread in the land of Martí; not the persecution, hunger, and treason they find today. Cuba should be the bulwark of liberty and not a shameful link in the chain of despotism.

...The problem of the land, the problem of industrialization, the problem of housing, the problem of unemployment, the problem of education, and

the problem of the people's health: these are the six problems we would take immediate steps to solve, along with restoration of civil liberties and political democracy.

The landscape of social injustice

Eighty-five percent of the small farmers in Cuba pay rent and live under constant threat of being evicted from the land they till. More than half of our most productive land is in the hands of foreigners. In Oriente, the largest province, the lands of the United Fruit Company and the West Indian Company link the northern and southern coasts. There are two hundred thousand peasant families who do not have a single acre of land to till to provide food for their starving children. On the other hand, nearly three hundred thousand caballerías of cultivable land owned by powerful interests remain uncultivated. If Cuba is above all an agricultural State, if its population is largely rural, if the city depends on these rural areas, if the people from our countryside won our war of independence, if our nation's greatness and prosperity depend on a healthy and vigorous rural population that loves the land and knows how to work it, if this population depends on a State that protects and guides it, then how can the present state of affairs be allowed to continue?

Except for a few food, lumber, and textile industries, Cuba continues to be primarily a producer of raw materials. We export sugar to import candy, we export hides to import shoes, we export iron to import plows.

…Everyone agrees with the urgent need to industrialize the nation, that we need steel industries, paper, and chemical industries, that we must improve our cattle and grain production, the technology and processing in our food industry in order to defend ourselves against the ruinous competition from Europe in cheese products, condensed milk, liquors, and edible oils, and the United States in canned goods; that we need cargo ships; that tourism should be an enormous source of revenue. But the

capitalists insist that the workers remain under the yoke. The State sits back with its arms crossed and industrialization can wait forever.

Just as serious or even worse is the housing problem. There are two hundred thousand huts and hovels in Cuba; four hundred thousand families in the countryside and in the cities live cramped in huts and tenements without even the minimum sanitary requirements; 2.2 million of our urban population pay rents which absorb between one fifth and one third of their incomes; and 2.8 million of our rural and suburban population lack electricity.

…Our educational system is perfectly compatible with everything I've just mentioned. Where the peasant doesn't own the land, what need is there for agricultural schools? Where there is no industry, what need is there for technical or vocational schools? Everything follows the same absurd logic; if we don't have one thing we can't have the other.

Only death can liberate one from so much misery.

Only death can liberate one from so much misery. In this respect, however, the State is most helpful—in providing early death for the people. Ninety percent of the children in the countryside are consumed by parasites, which filter through their bare feet from the ground they walk on. Society is moved to compassion when it hears of the kidnapping or murder of one child, but it is indifferent to the mass murder of so many thousands of children who die every year from lack of facilities, agonizing with pain. Their innocent eyes, death already shining in them, seem to look into some vague infinity as if entreating forgiveness for human selfishness, as if asking God to stay His wrath. And when the head of a family works only four months a year, with what can he purchase clothing and medicine for his children? They will grow up with rickets, with not a single good tooth in their mouths by the time they reach thirty; they will have heard ten million speeches and will finally die of misery and deception. Public hospitals, which are always full, accept only patients recommended by some powerful politician who, in return, demands the votes of the unfortunate one and his family so that Cuba may continue forever in the same or worse condition.

No excuse for such poverty.

Cuba could easily provide for a population three times as great as it has now, so there is no excuse for the abject poverty of a single one of its present inhabitants. The markets should be overflowing with produce, pantries should be full, all hands should be working. This is not an inconceivable thought. What is inconceivable is that anyone should go to bed hungry while there is a single inch of unproductive land; that children should die for lack of medical attention; what is inconceivable is that 30 percent of our farm people cannot write their names and that 99 percent of them know nothing of Cuba's history. What is inconceivable is that the majority of our rural people are now living in worse circumstances than the Indians Columbus discovered in the fairest land that human eyes had ever seen.

My logic is the simple logic of the people.

Since this trial may, as you said, be the most important trial since we achieved our national sovereignty, what I say here will perhaps be lost in the silence which the dictatorship has tried to impose on me, but posterity will often turn its eyes to what you do here. Remember that today you are judging an accused man, but that you yourselves will be judged not once, but many times, as often as these days are submitted to scrutiny in the future. What I say here will be then repeated many times, not because it comes from my lips, but because the problem of justice is eternal and the people have a deep sense of justice above and beyond the hairsplitting of jurisprudence. The people wield simple but implacable logic, in conflict with all that is absurd and contradictory. Furthermore, if there is in this world a people that utterly abhors favoritism and inequality, it is the

Cuban people. To them, justice is symbolized by a maiden with a scale and a sword in her hands. Should she cower before one group and furiously wield that sword against another group, then, to the people of Cuba, the maiden of justice will seem nothing more than a prostitute brandishing a dagger. My logic is the simple logic of the people.

Rebellion, freedom, dignity: A history of political thinking

The right of rebellion against tyranny, Honorable Judges, has been recognized from the most ancient times to the present day by men of all creeds, ideas and doctrines.

It was so in the theocratic monarchies of remote antiquity. In China it was almost a constitutional principle that when a king governed rudely and despotically, he should be deposed and replaced by a virtuous prince.

The philosophers of ancient India upheld the principle of active resistance to arbitrary authority. They justified revolution and very often put their theories into practice. One of their spiritual leaders used to say that "an opinion held by the majority is stronger than the king himself. A rope woven of many strands is strong enough to hold a lion."

The city states of Greece and republican Rome not only admitted, but defended the meting out of violent death to tyrants.

In the Middle Ages, John Salisbury, in his Book of the Statesman, *says that when a prince does not govern according to law and degenerates into a tyrant, violent overthrow is legitimate and justifiable. He recommends for tyrants the dagger rather than poison.*

Saint Thomas Aquinas, in the Summa Theologica, *rejects the doctrine of tyrannicide, and yet upholds the thesis that tyrants should be overthrown by the people.*

Martin Luther proclaimed that when a government degenerates into a tyranny that violates the laws, its subjects are released from their obligations to obey. His disciple, Philipp Melanchthon, upholds the right of resistance when governments become despotic. Calvin, the outstanding thinker of the Reformation with regard to political ideas, postulates that people are entitled to take up arms to oppose any usurpation.

No less a man than Juan Mariana, a Spanish Jesuit during the reign of Philip II, asserts in his book, De Rege et Regis Institutione, *that when a governor usurps power, or even if he were elected, when he governs in a tyrannical manner, it is licit for a private citizen to exercise tyrannicide, either directly or through subterfuge with the least possible disturbance.*

The French writer, François Hotman, maintained that between the government and its subjects there is a bond or contract, and that the people may rise in rebellion against the tyranny of government when the latter violates that pact.

About the same time, a booklet—which came to be widely read—appeared under the title Vindiciae Contra Tyrannos, *and it was signed with the pseudonym Stephanus Junius Brutus. It openly declared that resistance to governments is legitimate when rulers oppress the people and that it is the duty of Honorable Judges to lead the struggle.*

The Scottish reformers John Knox and John Poynet upheld the same points of view. And in the most important book of that movement, George Buchanan stated that if a government achieved power without taking into account the consent of the people, or if a government rules their destiny in an unjust or arbitrary fashion, then that government becomes a tyranny and can be divested of power or, in a final recourse, its leaders can be put to death.

John Althus, a German jurist of the early seventeenth century, stated in his Treatise on Politics *that sovereignty as the supreme authority of the State is born from the voluntary concourse of all its members; that governmental authority stems from the people and that its unjust, illegal, or tyrannical function exempts them from the duty of obedience and justifies resistance or rebellion.*

Thus far, Honorable Judges, I have mentioned examples from antiquity, from the Middle Ages, and from the beginnings of our times. I selected these examples from writers of all creeds. What is more, you can see that the right to rebellion is at the very root of Cuba's existence as a nation. By virtue of it, you are today able to appear in the robes of Cuban Judges. Would it be that those garments really served the cause of justice!

It is well known that in England during the seventeenth century, two kings, Charles I and James II, were dethroned for despotism. These actions coincided with the birth of liberal political philosophy and provided the ideological base for a new social class, which was then struggling to break the bonds of feudalism. Against divine right autocracies, this new philosophy upheld the principle of the social contract and of the consent of the governed, and constituted the foundation of the English Revolution of 1688, the American Revolution of 1775, and the French Revolution of 1789. These great revolutionary events ushered in the liberation of the Spanish colonies in the New World—the final link in that chain being broken by Cuba. The new philosophy nurtured our own political ideas and helped us to evolve our Constitutions, from the Constitution of Guáimaro up to the Constitution of 1940. The latter was influenced by the socialist currents of our time; the principle of the social function of property and of man's inalienable right to a decent living were built into it, although large vested interests have prevented fully enforcing those rights.

The right of insurrection against tyranny then underwent its final consecration and became a fundamental tenet of political liberty.

As far back as 1649, John Milton wrote that political power lies with the people, who can enthrone and dethrone kings and have the duty of overthrowing tyrants.

John Locke, in his essay on government, maintained that when the natural rights of man are violated, the people have the right and the duty to alter or abolish the government. "The only remedy against unauthorized force is opposition to it by force."

Jean-Jacques Rousseau said with great eloquence in his Social Contract, *"While a people sees itself forced to obey and obeys, it does well; but as soon as it can shake off the yoke and shakes it off, it does better, recovering its liberty through the use of the very right that has been taken away from it...The strongest man is never strong enough to be master forever, unless he converts force into right and obedience into duty. Force is a physical power; I do not see what morality one may derive from its use. To yield to force is an act of necessity, not of will; at the very least, it is an act of prudence. In what sense should this be called a duty?...To renounce freedom is to renounce one's status as a man, to renounce one's human rights, including one's duties. There is no possible compensation for renouncing everything. Total renunciation is incompatible with the nature of man and to take away all free will is to take away all morality of conduct. In short, it is vain and contradictory to stipulate on the one hand an absolute authority and on the other an unlimited obedience."*

Thomas Paine said that "one just man deserves more respect than a rogue with a crown."

The people's right to rebel has been opposed only by reactionaries like that clergyman of Virginia, Jonathan Boucher, who said: "The right to rebel is a censurable doctrine derived from Lucifer, the father of rebellions."

The Declaration of Independence of the Congress of Philadelphia, on July 4, 1776, consecrated this right in a beautiful paragraph which reads, "We hold these truths to be self-evident, that all men are created equal, that they are endowed by their Creator with certain inalienable rights, that among these are Life, Liberty and the Pursuit of Happiness; That to secure these Rights, Governments are instituted among Men, deriving their just powers from the consent of the governed; That whenever any Form of Government becomes destructive of these ends, it is the Right of the People to alter or abolish it and to institute a new Government, laying its foundation on such principles and organizing its powers in such form as to them shall seem most likely to affect their Safety and Happiness."

The famous French Declaration of the Rights of Man willed this principle to the coming generations: "When the government violates the rights of the people, insurrection is for them the most sacred of rights and the most imperative of duties. When a person seizes sovereignty, he should be condemned to death by free men."

...I know that imprisonment will be harder for me than it has ever been for anyone, filled with cowardly threats and hideous cruelty. But I do not fear prison, as I do not fear the fury of the miserable tyrant who took the lives of seventy of my comrades. Condemn me. It does not matter.

Appendix 2. The Monroe Doctrine

(Excerpted from President James Monroe, seventh annual message to Congress, December 2, 1823; for the full text see http://millercenter.org/president/speeches/detail/3604.)

At the proposal of the Russian Imperial Government, made through the minister of the Emperor residing here, a full power and instructions have been transmitted to the Minister of the United States at St. Petersburg to arrange, by amicable negotiation, the respective rights and interests of the two nations on the northwest coast of this continent. A similar proposal has been made by His Imperial Majesty to the Government of Great Britain, which has likewise been acceded to. The Government of the United States has been desirous, by this friendly proceeding, of manifesting the great value which they have invariably attached to the friendship of the Emperor, and their solicitude to cultivate the best understanding with his Government. In the discussions to which this interest has given rise, and in the arrangements by which they may terminate the occasion has been judged proper for asserting, as a principle in which the rights and interests of the United States are involved, that the American continents, by the free and independent condition which they have assumed and maintain, are henceforth not to be considered as subjects for future colonization by any European powers.

...It was stated at the commencement of the last session that a great effort was then making in Spain and Portugal, to improve the condition

of the people of those countries, and that it appeared to be conducted with extraordinary moderation. It need scarcely be remarked that the result has been, so far, very different from what was then anticipated. Of events in that quarter of the globe, with which we have so much intercourse, and from which we derive our origin, we have always been anxious and interested spectators. The citizens of the United States cherish sentiments the most friendly, in favor of the liberty and happiness of their fellow men on that side of the Atlantic. In the wars of the European powers, in matters relating to themselves, we have never taken any part, nor does it comport with our policy to do so. It is only when our rights are invaded, or seriously menaced, that we resent injuries, or make preparation for our defense. With the movements in this hemisphere, we are, of necessity, more immediately connected, and by causes which must be obvious to all enlightened and impartial observers. The political system of the allied powers is essentially different, in this respect, from that of America. This difference proceeds from that which exists in their respective governments. And to the defense of our own, which has been achieved by the loss of so much blood and treasure, and matured by the wisdom of their most enlightened citizens, and under which we have enjoyed unexampled felicity, this whole nation is devoted. We owe it, therefore, to candor, and to the amicable relations existing between the United States and those powers to declare that we should consider any attempt on their part to extend their system to any portion of this hemisphere as dangerous to our peace and safety. With the existing colonies or dependencies of any European power we have not interfered and shall not interfere. But with the governments who have declared their independence and maintained it, and whose independence we have, on great consideration and on just principles acknowledged, we could not view any interposition for the purpose of oppressing them, or controlling in any other manner, their destiny, by any European power in any other light than as the manifestation of an unfriendly disposition toward the United States. In the war between those new governments and Spain, we declared our neutrality at the time of their recognition, and to this we have adhered, and shall continue to adhere, provided no change shall occur, which, in the judgment of the competent authorities of this government, shall make a corresponding change on the part of the United States, indispensable to their security.

The late events in Spain and Portugal show that Europe is still unsettled. Of this important fact, no stronger proof can be adduced than that the allied powers should have thought it proper on any principle satisfactory to themselves to have interposed, by force, in the internal concerns of Spain. To what extent such interposition may be carried on the same principle is a question, to which all independent powers, whose governments differ from theirs, are interested; even those most remote, and surely none more so than the United States. Our policy, in regard to Europe, which was adopted at an early stage of the wars, which have so long agitated that quarter of the globe, nevertheless remains the same, which is not to interfere in the internal concerns of any of its powers; to consider the government de facto as the legitimate government for us; to cultivate friendly relations with it and to preserve those relations by a frank, firm, and manly policy; meeting, in all instances, the just claims of every power; submitting to injuries from none. But in regard to these continents, circumstances are eminently and conspicuously different. It is impossible that the allied powers should extend their political system to any portion of either continent without endangering our peace and happiness nor can anyone believe that our southern brethren, if left to themselves, would adopt it of their own accord. It is equally impossible, therefore, that we should behold such interposition, in any form, with indifference. If we look to the comparative strength and resources of Spain and those new governments, and their distance from each other, it must be obvious that she can never subdue them. It is still the true policy of the United States to leave the parties to themselves, in the hope that other powers will pursue the same course.

Appendix 3: Laws and Regulations

CUBAN ADJUSTMENT ACT, 1966, AND IIRIRA, 1996
(Overview provided by the American Immigration Law Center)

The Cuban Adjustment Act of 1966 (CAA) provides for a special procedure under which Cuban natives or citizens and their accompanying spouses and children may obtain a haven in the United States as lawful permanent residents. The CAA gives the attorney general the discretion to grant permanent residence to Cuban natives or citizens seeking adjustment of status if they have been present in the United States for at least one year after admission or parole and are admissible as immigrants. Their applications for adjustment of status may be approved even if they do not meet the ordinary requirements for adjustment of status under section 245 of the Immigration and Nationality Act. Since the caps on immigration do not apply to adjustments under the CAA, it is not necessary for the alien to be the beneficiary of a family-based or employment-based immigrant visa petition.

On September 30, 1996, Congress enacted the Illegal Immigration Reform and Immigrant Responsibility Act (IIRIRA). IIRIRA made several comprehensive changes to the immigration laws. In particular, IIRIRA stated that arrival in the United States at a place other than an open port of entry is a ground of inadmissibility. However, after serious consideration of IIRIRA, it was established that a Cuban native or citizen who arrives at a place other than an open port of entry may still be eligible for adjustment of status if paroled into the United States.

Eligibility: Cuban natives or citizens can apply for adjustment of status if they have been present in the United States for at least one year since admission or parole and are admissible as immigrants. The public charge ground of inadmissibility does not apply to applicants filing for benefits under the Cuban Adjustment Act. Nor does inadmissibility for having arrived at a place other than an open port of entry apply. A Cuban native or citizen who arrives at a place other than an open port of entry, therefore, is still eligible for adjustment of status as long as he or she has been paroled. If the applicant is inadmissible on any other ground, the applicant is not eligible for adjustment under the CAA unless the applicant is eligible for, and has obtained, a waiver of inadmissibility.

Information on Family Members: The CAA applies to the alien's spouse and children regardless of their country of citizenship or place of birth, provided:

- *the relationship continues to exist until the dependent spouse or child adjusts status;*
- *they are residing with the principal alien in the United States;*
- *they make an application for adjustment of status under the Cuban Adjustment Act;*
- *they are eligible to receive an immigrant visa; and*
- *they are otherwise admissible to the United States for such permanent residence.*

Note that the Immigration and Nationality Act defines "child" so that a person's son or daughter must be unmarried and not yet twenty-one years old to qualify. Stepchildren, adopted children, and children born out of wedlock can qualify if the claimed parent-child relationship meets the requirements specified in section 101(b)(1) of the Immigration and Nationality Act.

Cuban Refugee Program, 1972

(Excerpted from letter to John D. Twiname, Administrator, Social and Rehabilitation Service, Department of Health, Education, and Welfare, from the US General Accounting Office, March 22, 1972)

We have reviewed the Cuban refugee program administered by your agency within the Department of Health, Education, and Welfare (HEW).

On November 3, 1971, we issued a report entitled "Analysis of Federal Expenditures on Aid Cuban Refugees" (B-164031(3)) to the Subcommittee to Investigate Problems Connected with Refugees and Escapees, Senate Committee on the Judiciary.

This letter report—based on our review at HEW headquarters and at local welfare offices in two metropolitan areas—presents our views that certain HEW policies concerning the States providing public assistance to Cuban refugees are in need of clarification.

Introduction

When Fidel Castro came to power in Cuba early in 1959, thousands of Cuban people fled that country and many of them came to the United States, principally to the Miami area. Most of the refugees left all personal belongs in Cuba and arrived with virtually no money or resources.

Initially emergency assistance to meet the needs of the refugees was furnished by local public and private welfare organizations. In December 1960, however, the president established a Cuban Refugee Emergency

Center in Miami to relieve the mounting economic and social problems created by the heavy influx of refugees in that area. In February 1961, the president directed that a Cuban refugee program be established in HEW.

Permanent authority for the program was provided by the Migration and Refugee Assistance Act of 1962 (22 U.S.C 2601), which provides for (1) financial assistance to needy refugees, (2) financial assistance to State and local public agencies which provide services for substantial numbers of refugees, (3) paying the costs of resettling refugees from Miami, and (4) establishing employment and professional refresher training courses for refugees.

About 611,000 Cuban refugees have entered the United States since Fidel Castro came to power, of which about 443,000 have registered with the Cuban refugee program. A refugee remains eligible to receive services provided by the program until he attains US citizenship.

Public Assistance Payments

Public assistance is made available to needy Cuban refugees through the state public welfare departments. The states are reimbursed completely by the Cuban refugee program for their medical and assistance payments to, or on behalf of, refugees who qualify under the states' eligibility standards. The level of public assistance payments received by refugees varies from state to state, depending on the state's benefit level for its regular public assistance recipients.

Cuban refugee program officials estimate that public assistance and medical payments will amount to about $107 million in fiscal 1972, and that about 90,000 refugees will be receiving some form of public assistance by the end of fiscal 1972.

President Kennedy, in February 1961, established the Cuban refugee program in HEW to assist needy refugees based on standards used in the community involved. The Cuban refugee program policies provide for aiding those refugees who are in urgent need of assistance for the essentials of life. HEW's policies to states providing assistance to needy Cuban refugees—issued in August 1962 and currently in effect—require that the standards used in determining the extent of help to be provided be in keeping with those used by the public welfare agency of the State to which the Cuban refugee is resettled.

The program further defines this general policy by providing that needy families with children under eighteen will be granted assistance in accordance with state standards under the program for aid to families with dependent children (AFDC). In adult cases (aged, blind, disabled) the state public assistance standards which are most appropriate in meeting the refugee's needs are to be used. The program also requires that the full range of social services available to regular public assistance recipients be furnished to eligible Cuban refugees.

On numerous occasions during congressional appropriations hearings, Cuban refugee program officials have reiterated their intent of providing refugees with public assistance benefits on the same basis as that provided to needy Americans.

Granting of Benefits Different from Those Provided to Regular Program Beneficiaries

In two locations visited by us—Los Angeles, California, and Boston, Massachusetts—the local welfare agencies are following policies which we believe are contrary to the intent of the Cuban refugee program in that refugees are receiving benefits lower (Boston) and higher (Los Angeles) than those received by the states' regular welfare recipients.

...We believe that needy refugees in Los Angeles County—not eligible for benefits under the federally assisted programs authorized by the Social Security Act—should be paid at the general relief program levels, and not at levels paid to persons eligible for benefits under the [local] program. The same would apply to any county in the United States where a general relief program was in operation. We recognize that, in those states or counties which do not have general relief programs, substitutions of levels used in the federally assisted programs might be necessary and administratively desirable.

...Massachusetts regulations covering its AFDC program provide that a family, upon initial determination of eligibility, is entitled to receive

(1) new household equipment, supplies, and furniture if needed, (2) the regular monthly assistance payment, (3) emergency assistance in the event of extreme hardship situations, and (4) a regular quarterly grant to meet special needs, such as seasonal clothing, repairs to appliances, etc. Cuban refugee families are entitled to all of the aforementioned benefits except the quarterly grant. This grant amounts to about $105 per quarter for a family of four.

An official of the Massachusetts Department of Public Welfare explained to us that Cuban refugee families do not receive the quarterly grant since they receive higher initial assistance for household equipment, supplies, and furniture than most other AFDC families.

We believe that refugees [in Boston] should be receiving the grants according to the HEW criteria that Cuban refugees are to receive the same public assistance benefits as are received by US citizens.

Similar situations may exist in other states. To avoid the charge that the Cuban refugee program is discriminatory, we believe that HEW should clarify its policies covering public assistance benefits paid to Cuban refugees by state letter specifying that needy refugees be granted assistance based on standards used in the county or state involved for other public assistance recipients.

Cuban Democracy Act, 1992

This law prohibited foreign-based subsidiaries of US companies from trading with Cuba, prohibited travel to Cuba by US citizens, and prohibited family remittances to Cuba. Its stated objective was to "promote a peaceful transition to democracy in Cuba through the application of sanctions directed at the Castro government and support for the Cuban people." The act noted that Castro's government "demonstrated consistent disregard for internationally accepted standards of human rights and for democratic values."

Cuban Migration Lottery, 1994

Three entry periods have occurred: 1994 (189,000 registrants), 1996 (433,000), and 1998 (541,000). In 2015, Cubans that qualified in the 1998 lottery are still being processed into the United States. Persons interested in immigrating to the United States apply for the lottery by providing a letter to the US Interests Section during the specified entry period. The last entry period was from June 15, 1998, to July 15, 1998. The next entry period has not been scheduled at this time. During lottery-entry periods, entries are received through the Cuban mail system at the US Interests Section. Applications thus received are forwarded to Washington for processing.

In Washington, all entries are data-entered and potential winners are randomly selected. All potential winners are rank-ordered in Washington, and potential winners' application packets are prepared and sent to the US

Interests Section. The Interests Section contacts applicants for interviews starting from the top of the list throughout the fiscal year. These applicants are mailed letters that contain instructions and forms and describe the documents required for an interview. The letters also invite the applicants to call the Interests Section and schedule an interview once all the required documents have been gathered. The number of letters mailed to successful entrants is based on estimates of the number of approved immigrants needed to complete the target of twenty thousand at the end of the fiscal year as established by the US-Cuban Migration Accord. Estimates are revised continually throughout the fiscal year, and the number of letters mailed is adjusted accordingly.

Each lottery winner who contacts the Interests Section receives an appointment to be interviewed at the Consular Section. While the winners are admitted based on the attorney general's parole authority rather than as regular immigrants, they must nevertheless establish that they are not ineligible for admission under US law, including that they have not been convicted of serious crimes, are not members of a terrorist organization, and will not become public charges.

Winning the lottery does not guarantee the applicant's admission; rather it provides an opportunity to be interviewed for consideration under the parole authority. The individual must meet at least two of the three basic qualifications for this program (high school education, three or more years' work experience, relatives living in the United States). Persons in the United States who wish to provide affidavits of support on behalf of winners of the Cuban lottery of the worldwide Diversity Visa lottery should note that the Form I-864 cannot be accepted for these types of cases. The proper form to use to provide an affidavit of support for all parole and Diversity Visa cases is the Form I-134.

Helms-Burton Act (or Libertad Act), 1996

Properly called the Cuban Liberty and Democratic Solidarity Act of 1996, this law strengthened and continued the US embargo against Cuba. It extended the embargo to apply to foreign companies trading with Cuba and penalized them for "trafficking" in expropriated property. Nicknamed for sponsors Senator Jesse Helms and Representative Dan Burton, the bill was tabled in 1995 but reintroduced after Cuban fighter jets, in February 1996, shot down two airplanes operated by a Miami-based refugee support group. The law passed on March 12, 1996.

The Myth of Helms-Burton: Why the President Can Change the Rules Governing US-Cuba Policy

Jake Colvin

(Colvin is vice president for global trade issues at the National Foreign Trade Council, which promotes open and fair global markets; this report is adapted from his "The Case for a New Cuba Policy," available at www.usaengage.org.)

Widespread speculation that the Obama administration will loosen restrictions on the ability of American citizens to travel to Cuba has renewed questions about the authority of the president to alter Cuba policy.

Some have argued that even if President Obama is inclined to change policy, Congress has tied his hands by passing legislation on Cuba. While Congress has a significant role to play in ending the attack on the right of US citizens to travel freely to Cuba, the administration's hands are far from tied when it comes to shaping policy.

Current Executive Branch Discretion

In codifying the embargo, "including all restrictions under part 515 of title 31," Congress captured in Helms-Burton the president's discretion to change the restrictions. This licensing authority is stated throughout the Cuban Assets Control Regulations (CACR). Section 201(a) and (b) and Section 204(a) specify that transactions involving Cuba are prohibited "except as specifically authorized by the Secretary of the Treasury (or any person, agency, or instrumentality designated by him) by means of regulations, rulings, instructions, licenses, or otherwise." Section 202 indicates that securities transactions with Cuban nationals are prohibited "unless authorized by a license expressly referring to this section." The regulations restrict holding blocked property "except…as authorized by the Secretary of the Treasury or his delegate by specific license."

Both Clinton and Bush utilized this discretion to modify the Cuba sanctions regulations following the passage of the Libertad Act in 1996. After Pope John Paul II visited Cuba in January 1998, the Clinton administration changed the rules to permit Cuban Americans to send money to relatives in Cuba and to allow direct flights between the United States and Havana. On January 5, 1999, Clinton announced that his administration would expand remittances to Cuba; increase people-to-people exchanges with Cuban academics, athletes, and scientists; and allow sales of agricultural products to independent groups in Cuba.

In 2008, the Bush administration announced and published regulations to permit Cuban Americans to distribute cell phones to relatives on the island. In explaining the policy, NSC Senior Director for Western Hemisphere Affairs Dan Fisk said, "In this case, the State Department and the Department of Commerce will work together to change the regulatory structure. It's a Federal Register [notice]…Most of the embargo is actually contained in federal regulations." (Oddly, the Bush administration used its discretion to exempt US-origin electronics on the Commerce Control List, which are specially controlled by the Department of Commerce for reasons of antiterrorism, to a country that the State Department says is a sponsor of terrorism.)

The Trade Sanctions Reform and Export Enhancement Act of 2000

Ironically, the only piece of legislation that may restrict executive authority is the one that was designed to loosen the trade embargo. In 2000, a bipartisan group of lawmakers helped enact the Trade Sanctions Reform and Export Enhancement Act (TSRA). The law exempts exports of food, medicine, medical products, and agricultural products from US sanctions. It is because of TSRA that US farmers can sell lentils and poultry to Cuba and medicine and defibrillators to Sudan and the Palestinian Authority.

In exchange for exempting humanitarian trade from the embargo, pro-embargo members of Congress championed a provision that prohibits the executive branch from licensing "travel to, from, or within Cuba for tourist activities." The president may only license travel under a dozen categories of purposeful travel, which are contained in Section 515.560 of the Cuban Assets Control Regulations. They are:

(1.) Family visits;
(2.) Official business of the US government, foreign governments, and certain intergovernmental organizations;
(3.) Journalistic activity;
(4.) Professional research;
(5.) Educational activities;
(6.) Religious activities;
(7.) Public performances, clinics, workshops, athletic and other competitions, and exhibitions;
(8.) Support for the Cuban people;
(9.) Humanitarian projects (specific licenses);
(10.) Activities of private foundations or research or educational institutes;
(11.) Exportation, importation, or transmission of information or informational materials; and
(12.) Certain export and marketing transactions.

As a result of TSRA, one of the most logical steps the president might wish to take—lifting the travel ban—would likely require an act of Congress.

How President Obama Can Expand Travel to Cuba

At the same time, the president retains a great deal of discretion within these categories to increase people-to-people contact with Cuba. First, the administration can loosen the qualifications under the various categories of travel. For example, the Bush administration imposed a condition that, in order to travel to Cuba under an academic license, a student had to be enrolled in a degree program and engaged in study in Cuba that was no shorter than ten weeks. President Bush also prohibited visits, which were allowed under Clinton administration policies, by individuals to Cuba when a family member is in Cuba pursuant to an OFAC license, except in "exigent" circumstances and only "after consultation with the Department of State, in true emergency situations, such as serious illness accompanied by an inability to travel." Loosening these and other rules could have a significant impact on travel to Cuba.

Another change that could have a significant impact would be to permit more travel to Cuba via general licenses rather than requiring specific license applications. The administration currently relies heavily on "specific licenses," which requires the Treasury Department to approve individual applications to travel to Cuba in many cases.

The administration should ease the burden on the Treasury Department by mandating general licensing of authorized categories of travel to Cuba while redeploying resources internally to focus on the department's urgent priorities of tracking terrorist financing. Loosening travel restrictions would be a welcome step in the right direction that would create additional momentum for Congress to end the entire travel ban.

Endnotes

CHAPTER 1. ONE CONCLUSION, TWO PATHS

1. http://www.whitehouse.gov/the-press-office/2014/12/17/fact-sheet-charting-new-course-cuba.

2. Camagüey today has 305,000 people. Greater Havana is a city of some 3 million, while Santiago de Cuba has a population of some 600,000, and Miami's Cuban population falls in between. See Jesús Arboleya, "The Cuban American Enclave in Miami," *Progreso Weekly*, November 6, 2013, http://progresoweekly.us/cuban-american-enclave-miami/.

CHAPTER 2. FROM CAMAGÜEY TO EXILE

1. The five-story El Encanto was Cuba's largest department store. It was built in 1888, nationalized in 1959, and destroyed by fire in 1961 following an arson attack using explosives provided by the CIA. It was located in Old Havana at the corner of Galiano and San Rafael; the site has since become a park. See Juan Carlos Rodriguez, *The Bay of Pigs and the CIA* (New York: Ocean Press, 1999).

2. *Sofrito* is the foundation of Cuban cuisine: a purée of tomatoes, peppers, onions, and garlic.

3. *Turrones* are nougat confections made of sugar or honey and egg white; *puerco asado* is roast pork; *mojito* is a marinating sauce made of lime, garlic, sour orange, and other spices.

4. Fidel Castro, *History Will Absolve Me* (New York: Lyle Stuart, 1961). The extended 1953 speech *La historia me absolverá* was part of his defense when on trial for a failed rebellion against the Batista regime. The complete speech is available in the Castro Internet Archive at http://www.marxists.org/history/cuba/archive/castro/1953/10/16.htm.

5. In the Catholic Church, an indulgence is a means whereby you reduce your sins. Indulgences are granted for prayers and good deeds performed with appropriate devotion. I attended a Catholic school where the sisters taught us about this, and I counted my indulgence every day. I literally kept a little notebook counting how many points I had accumulated in indulgence in order to enter heaven.

CHAPTER 3. LATIN AMERICAN JOURNEY FROM REDNECK TO YUMA

1. The Gulf of Tonkin resolution gave the US president the authority to broaden the scope of the war in Vietnam.

2. J. William Fulbright, *The Arrogance of Power* (New York: Random House, 1967).

3. In 1961 the Sandinista National Liberation Front (Frente Sandinista de Liberación Nacional) was founded by Silvio Mayorga, Tomás Borge, and Carlos Fonseca. The group took its name from Augusto Cesár Sandino, who led a Liberal peasant army against the government of US-backed Adolfo Díaz and the subsequent Nicaraguan government in the late 1920s and early 1930s. Inspired by Fidel Castro, Che Guevara, and the Cuban Revolution, the group sought to be "a political-military organization whose objective [was] the seizure of political power through the destruction of the bureaucratic and military apparatus of [Somoza's] dictatorship" ("The Sandinistas," Understanding the Iran-Contra Affairs, http://www.brown.edu/Research/Understanding_the_Iran_Contra_Affair/n-sandinistas.php).

4. Kirby Jones has traveled regularly to Cuba for the last three decades, has consulted with dozens of US firms and organizations, has conducted several television and print interviews with Fidel Castro, and has written extensively about Cuba. Described by *Newsweek* as

having "better contacts in Cuba than any other American," and by the *New York Times* as the "man to see about business in Cuba," Jones is the president of Alamar, a Maryland-based consulting firm that provides a full range of consulting services to companies and organizations interested in establishing relationships with and conducting business in Cuba (Alamar Associates, http://www.alamar-cuba.com/).

CHAPTER 4. CUBA MATTERS

1. United Nations 68th General Assembly, press release, GA-11445, October 19, 2013.

2. http://www.unmultimedia.org/oralhistory/2013/03/montano-jorge/.

3. Ana Maria Benedetti, "Latin American Leaders Cheer Historic Opening of US-Cuba Relations," *Huffington Post*, December 17, 2014, http://www.huffingtonpost.com/2014/12/17/leaders-in-latin-america-_n_6343524.html.

CHAPTER 5. NEW DYNAMICS

1. Lincoln Diaz-Balart, former congressman for Miami, interview by Alberto de la Cruz, *Miami Herald*, April 26, 2013.

2. http://www.whitehouse.gov/the-press-office/2014/12/17/fact-sheet-charting-new-course-cuba.

3. "Speech by Cuban President Raúl Castro on Re-establishing US-Cuba Relations" (translation), *Washington Post*, December 17, 2014, http://www.washingtonpost.com/world/full-text-speech-by-cuban-president-raul-castro-on-re-establishing-us-cuba-relations/2014/12/17/45bc2f88-8616-11e4-b9b7-b8632ae73d25_story.html.

4. "Lawmakers Split over US Plan to Normalize Cuba Relations," *Wall Street Journal*, December 18, 2014, http://www.wsj.com/articles/lawmakers-split-over-u-s-plan-to-normalize-cuba-relations-1418844782.

5. www.menendez.senate.gov.

6. *Wall Street Journal*, December 18, 2014.

7. http://www.whitehouse.gov/the-press-office/2014/12/17/fact-sheet-charting-new-course-cuba.

CHAPTER 6. HISTORICAL DISCORD

1. President James Monroe, seventh annual message to Congress, December 2, 1823, full text at http://millercenter.org/president/speeches/detail/3604.

2. US Department of State, Office of the Historian, "Milestones: 1899–1913, Roosevelt Corollary to the Monroe Doctrine, 1904," http://history.state.gov/milestones/1899-1913/roosevelt-and-monroe-doctrine.

3. Quoted in Charles Sellers, *The Market Revolution* (New York: Oxford University Press, 1991), 100.

4. George B. Young, "Intervention under the Monroe Doctrine: The Olney Corollary," *Political Science Quarterly* 57, no. 2 (June 1942): 247–80.

5. *Mambises* (plural of *mambi*) were heroes to the Cuban people as Cuban guerrillas in both the war of 1868–78 and the 1895 War of Independence; interestingly, they urged slaves to join the struggle (http://www.loc.gov/rr/hispanic/1898/mambises.html).

6. Treaty of Peace between the United States and Spain, December 10, 1898, http://avalon.law.yale.edu/19th_century/sp1898.asp.

7. Cesar J. Ayala, "Social and Economic Aspects of Sugar Production in Cuba, 1880-1930," *Latin American Research Review* 30, no. 1 (1995): 95–124.

8. See appendix B in Richard Gott, *Cuba: A New History* (New Haven, Conn.: Yale University Press, 2004).

9. Quoted in Gott, *Cuba*, 108.

10. Message from General Woodford to the President of the United States, March 17, 1898, cited in Louis A. Pérez Jr., *Cuba and the United States* (Athens: University of Georgia Press, 2003), 291, note 27.

11. timelinesdb.com.

CHAPTER 7. MIAMI MANIA

1. Castro's *History Will Absolve Me* speech is widely available in numerous editions in English and Spanish. The full text is in the Castro Internet Archive at http://www.marxists.org/history/cuba/archive/castro/1953/10/16.htm.

2. The Freedom Flights represented the largest and longest resettlement program of political refugees ever sponsored by the US government, offering 265,000 people an escape from Fidel Castro's Cuba (*Miami Herald*, December 12, 2008).

3. Our division of immigrants into three great waves (the Old Guard up to 1973, the Marielitos in 1980, and those who came under visa quotas in the 1990s) is an oversimplification. Several waves of smaller scale

occurred, such as Operation Peter Pan in 1960–62, which brought some 14,000 children, and the Camarioca boatlift of 1965; there have also been ongoing arrivals of *balseros* (rafters).

4. The wet foot/dry foot policy revision provides that Cuban refugees reaching the United States are allowed to pursue US residency. After talks with the Cuban government, the Clinton Administration came to an agreement with Cuba to stop admitting people found at sea. Since then a Cuban found on the waters between the two nations (i.e., with "wet feet") is summarily sent home or to a third country. One who makes it to shore (i.e., with "dry feet") gets a chance to remain in the United States and later qualifies for expedited permanent resident status and eventually US citizenship.

The *bombo* or lottery is based on requests for parole under the Special Program for Cuban Migration. Because the total number of persons qualifying for immigrant visas and refugee status does not normally reach the 20,000 that the United States has authorized each year under the US-Cuban Migration Accords of 1994, a lottery system allows persons who do not qualify as refugees or immigrants to seek US entry. This system is unique to Cuba and separate from the worldwide diversity visa lottery, for which Cubans are also eligible. See appendix 4 for more about how the lottery program works.

5. *Resolver* means to survive, to sort things out, finding a solution to everyday problems.

6. Earl Shorris, *Latinos: A Biography of the People* (New York: W. W. Norton, 2012).

7. See www2.fiu.edu/~morenod/scholar/empower.htm.

8. "US-Cuba Democracy PAC Announces 'Young Leaders Group,'" July 30, 2013, http://www.capitolhillcubans.com/2013/07/us-cuba-democracy-pac-announces-young.html. The Young Leaders Group plays a key role in the PAC's policy discussions, community outreach, and social media. It consists of dynamic young professional and student leaders (under thirty-five) with a proven commitment to democracy, human rights, and the rule of law. "The passion and enthusiasm of these young leaders...proves that we are passing the torch with a stronger flame than ever," said PAC Treasurer Gus Machado.

   Their agenda includes issue advocacy: "The YLG will continue to advocate for a US policy that holds paramount the fundamental right of the Cuban people to be free and enjoy all liberties." On the founding Board of Directors are members from Miami, Washington, Philadelphia, and Atlanta: human-rights advocate Anthony Cruz; Keith Fernandez, former campaign advisor to Representative Ileana Ros-Lehtinen; attorney Carlos M. Gutierrez Jr., a former aide to Congressman Mario Díaz-Balart; Florida lawyer Gregory Hernandez; civil trial attorney Marco Leyte-Vidal; University of Miami law student Vanessa Lopez, a founding member of Students for a Free Cuba; and Georgetown law student Rudy Mayor.

9. Quoted in David B. Truman, *The Governmental Process* (New York: Alfred A. Knopf, 1962).

10. Adam Smith, "Hard-Line Cuban American Money Flows to Congress," November 16, 2009, http://www.publicampaign.org/pressroom/2009/11/16/cuba-report. Based in Washington, DC, Public Campaign is a national nonprofit organization dedicated to advancing comprehensive reform of America's election laws.

11. Lincoln Díaz-Balart, former congressman for Miami, interview by Alberto de la Cruz, *Miami Herald*, April 26, 2013.

12. Florida Bill 959 (CS/CS/HB 959), State and Local Government Relations with Cuba or Syria. The vote was 39-1 in the State Senate and 115-0 in the State House. If approved by the governor, the provisions were to take effect on July 1, 2012. According to a summary prepared by the Governmental Oversight and Accountability Committee, the bill prohibited the State Board of Administration (SBA) from serving as a fiduciary with respect to voting for expanded US trade with Cuba or Syria, and prohibited SBA from voting to expand United States trade with Cuba or Syria. It also prohibited a company with business operations in Cuba or Syria from bidding on or entering into a contract with an agency or local governmental entity for goods or services of one million dollars or more.

13. Peter Wallsten and Tom Hamburger, "Sugar Protections Prove Easy to Swallow for Lawmakers across Political Spectrum," *Washington Post*, December 7, 2013, http://www.washingtonpost.com.

CHAPTER 8. PASSION, PERSISTENCE, AND PATIENCE

1. Pope John Paul II, speech on arrival in Cuba, January 21, 1998; and see http://news.bbc.co.uk/onthisday/hi/dates/stories/january/25/newsid_4041000/4041643.stm.

2. Pope John Paul II, farewell speech, Havana, January 25, 1998.

3. "Pope Benedict Meets Raúl Castro at Start of Cuba Visit," BBC News, March 27, 2012, http://www.bbc.com/news/world-latin-america-17509340.

4. *Cubano de a pie* is a phrase applied to Cubans on the island who struggle for their daily living and receive no remittances.

5. *El Período Especial* was an extended period of economic crisis that began in 1991 after the dissolution of the Soviet Union and its Council for Mutual Economic Assistance (Comecon), the Soviet equivalent of

the Organization for European Economic Co-Opera...
Europe. The depression of the Special Period was at its ...
the early to mid-1990s before slightly declining in severity ...
end of the decade. It was defined primarily by severe shorta... ...f hy-
drocarbon-energy resources in the form of gasoline, diesel, and other
petroleum derivatives that occurred upon the implosion of economic agreements between the petroleum-rich Soviet Union and Cuba.
The period radically transformed Cuban society and the economy, as
it necessitated successful introduction of sustainable agriculture and
decreased use of automobiles; it overhauled industry, health, and diet
countrywide as people were forced to make do.

6. See www.cubagob.cu.

7. *CIA World Factbook*: China, https://www.cia.gov/library/publications/
    the-world-factbook/geos/ch.html.

8. Larry Rohter, "The Pope in Cuba," *New York Times*, January 28, 1998,
    http://www.nytimes.com/1998/01/26/world/the-pope-in-cuba-the-
    overview-pope-asks-cubans-to-seek-new-path-toward-freedom.html.

9. CubaNews, March 7, 2001.

10. See Alabama-Cuba Initiative, University of Alabama College of Arts
    and Sciences, http://cuba.ua.edu/.

CHAPTER 9. POLITICS AND POLLOS

1. *Comandante* is how many Cubans have referred to Fidel Castro for decades.

2. US Senate, Committee on Finance, Baucus Secures Deal on Ag Sales
    to Cuba, press release, July 29, 2005, http://www.finance.senate.gov/
    newsroom/ranking/release/?id=ec243c25-b2c8-47f8-9a02-c13cb-
    24403be.

3. See Jonathan R. Coleman, "US Agricultural Sales to Cuba: Certain Economic Effects of US Restrictions," Office of Industries Working Paper no. ID-22, US International Trade Commission, June 2009, http://www.usitc.gov/publications/332/working_papers/ID-22.pdf.

CHAPTER 10. Y CUBA QUE?

1. "Havana's Unchanging Hardline," *Miami Herald*, February 16, 2014.

2. "United States Policy on Non-Recognition of Communist China, August 11, 1958," *Department of State Bulletin* 39 (September 8, 1958): 385–90.

3. Pewhispanic.org.

4. "Cuba, China Sign Trade Deals in Havana," CCTV English, September 28, 2012, http://english.cntv.cn/program/bizasia/20120928/102821.shtml.

5. Quoted in Mary Beth Sheridan, "US Is Urged to Ease Off Cuba," *Washington Post*, May 29, 2009, http://www.washingtonpost.com/wp-dyn/content/article/2009/05/28/AR2009052803766.html.

6. Jaime Suchlicki, "Keep US Sanctions on Cuba," *New York Times*, November 20, 2013. Suchlicki is a history professor, editor of *Cuban Affairs Journal*, director of Institute for Cuban and Cuban American Studies at the University of Miami, and author of *Cuba from Columbus to Castro* and *Breve Historia de Cuba*.

"No study of Eastern Europe or the Soviet Union claims that tourism, trade or investments had anything to do with the end of communism," notes Suchlicki. On whether engagement with a totalitarian state can bring about its demise, he says there is no evidence to support this:

Only academic ideologues and some members of Congress interested in catering to the economic needs of their state's constituencies cling to this notion. Their calls for ending the embargo have little to do with democracy in Cuba or the welfare of the Cuban people.

The repeated statement that the embargo is the cause of Cuba's economic problems is hollow. The reasons for the economic misery of the Cubans are a failed political and economic system. Like the communist systems of Eastern Europe, Cuba's system does not function, stifles initiative and productivity, and destroys human freedom and dignity... Normalization of relations with a military dictatorship in Cuba will send the wrong message to the rest of the continent.

If the travel ban and the embargo are ended unilaterally now by the United States, what will the US government have to negotiate with a future regime in Cuba and to encourage changes in the island?

7. These 1997 agreements involved Cuban holdings of International Telegraph and Telephone and the Italian telecommunications company STET; see Rolando Anillo-Baria, "Outstanding Claims to Expropriated Property in Cuba," http://www.ascecuba.org/publications/proceedings/volume21/pdfs/anillo.pdf.

8. Charlene M. Levie, "The Blocked Chinese Assets—United States Claims Problem: The Lump-Sum Settlement Solution," http://ir.lawnet.fordham.edu/ilj; see also http://history.state.gov/milestones/937-945/mexican-oil.

9. Quoted in Marc Lacey, "US and Cuba Work Together on Storms," *New York Times*, August 20, 2009.

10. Quoted in Albor Ruiz, "US and Cuba Improve Relations as Both Countries Aid in Relief Efforts in Haiti," *New York Daily News*, January 27, 2010.

11. See www.ustr.gov/countries-regions/americas/dominican-republic.

12. See www.cubaheadlines.com/2013/08/08/37768/travelers_to_cuba.

CHAPTER 11. AFTER THE EUPHORIA

1. Tina Rosenberg, *The Haunted Land* (New York: Random House, 1995).

2. Quoted in *Miami Herald*, December 22, 2013.

3. According to Article 89 of the Cuban Constitution, *El Consejo de Estado*, the State Council is the organ that represents the National Assembly of People's Power between legislative sessions, executing agreements and conducting such other functions as are assigned by the Constitution. All decisions of the State Council are adopted by the affirmative vote of a simple majority of its members (*Cubadebate*). Article 90 specifies the powers of the State Council to call special sessions of the National Assembly of People's Power; set National Assembly election dates; issue decree-laws between National Assembly sessions; provide interpretation of existing laws; exercise legislative initiative; and provide pertinent referendums by the National Assembly. The State Council also has the authority, when the National Assembly is in recess and cannot be convened urgently or securely, to decree general mobilization to defend the country when required, to declare war in case of aggression, or to make peace. Its further tasks are to replace members of the Council of Ministers if needed between National Assembly sessions; provide general instructions to the courts; instruct the attorney general; appoint and remove diplomatic representatives of Cuba to or from other States; grant decorations and honorary titles; appoint committees; grant pardons; ratify or denounce international treaties; grant or refuse recognition to diplomatic representatives of other states; suspend the provisions of the Council of Ministers and the agreements and provisions of Local Assemblies of People's Power that do not comply with the Constitution or the law, or when they affect the interests of other

localities or the country as a whole, reporting to the National Assembly accordingly in the first session held after the suspension; revoke the agreements and provisions of local bodies that infringe on the Constitution, laws, decree-laws, decrees, and other provisions issued by a higher body, or when affecting the interests of other localities or the nation; adopt rules of procedure; and "the other powers conferred by the Constitution and laws or granted by the National Assembly of People's Power."

4. Roger F. Noriega, "For Venezuelan Regime, the Party's Over," *American* (online magazine, American Enterprise Institute), February 18, 2014, http://www.american.com/archive/2014/february/for-venezuelan-regime-the-partys-over.

5. *Havana Time*, September 25, 2013.

6. See http://www.gao.gov/new.items/d07147.pdf.

7. Phillip Sherwell, "Welcome to Honduras, the Most Dangerous Country on the Planet," *Telegraph*, November 16, 2013.

8. *The Hill*, May 20, 2013.

CHAPTER 12. NO EXCUSES, BASTA YA

1. Mike Godfrey, "Cuba Celebrates Opening of Mariel Port," Tax-News.com (Washington), January 29, 2014, http://www.tax-news.com/news/Cuba_Celebrates_Opening_Of_Mariel_Port____63531.htm. See also http://pneumaticdetach.com/official-opening-of-super-port-cuban-mariel/.

2. "South Florida Ship First into Cuba's Mariel Mega-Port," *Hellenic ShippingNews,*February 4, 2014, http://www.hellenicshippingnews.com/News.aspx?ElementId=8c4201f0-d12d-484a-8e51-2e7db5accd9e.

3. "Address by President Dilma Rousseff, Inauguration Ceremony of the Port of Mariel, Province of Artemisa, Cuba, 27 January 2014," www. investorideas.com newswire, official translation, January 29, 2014, http://www.investorideas.com/news/2014/international/01291.asp.

4. "President Barack Obama's State of the Union Address," January 28, 2014, http://www.whitehouse.gov/the-press-office/2014/01/28/ president-barack-obamas-state-union-address.

5. Gertrude Stein, *Everybody's Autobiography* (New York: Random House, 1937), 289.

6. Margaret MacMillan, *The War That Ended Peace* (New York: Random House, 2013).

7. Peter Wallsten, Manuel Roig-Franzia, and Tom Hamburger, "Sugar Tycoon Alfonso Fanjul Now Open to Investing in Cuba under 'Right Circumstances,'" *Washington Post*, February 2, 2014. According to the *Post*, "Fanjul visited Cuba in April 2012 and again in February 2013 as part of a delegation licensed through the Brookings Institution, the Washington think tank that has produced recent papers criticizing US policy and calling on the Obama Administration to further loosen sanctions. In Havana, he lingered with tears in his eyes at his family's colonial-era manse, now a museum, with its elegant columns, lush inner courtyard, sparkling chandeliers, and grand staircase."

Political complexity puts him "on a potential collision course" with Senate Foreign Relations Committee Chair Robert Menéndez, a Cuban American who is a committed advocate for the embargo. "Trickier still would be the impact on presidential politics, with Florida's Cuban American electorate still a significant factor in the battle for that state's crucial electoral college votes." Yet younger Cuban Americans born in the United States are "moving away from the hard-line views of their parents and grandparents," notes the *Post*, and in their pursuit of Florida's large Cuban American electorate, politicians favoring the embargo "will have to calibrate the risks and rewards" of evolving with voters.

8. Wallsten et al., "Sugar Tycoon."

9. Wallsten et al., "Sugar Tycoon."

10. Wallsten et al., "Sugar Tycoon."

Jay Brickman—Bio

Jay Brickman is the vice president of government services for Crowley Liner Services. Crowley is a privately owned company that began operations in 1892. Today it is one of the most diversified shipping and logistics companies in the United States.

While presently based in Fort Lauderdale, Florida, Jay was previously stationed in Managua, Nicaragua; Panama City, Panama; San Juan, Puerto Rico; Caracas, Venezuela; and Mexico City, Mexico.

He has initiated and directed Crowley's operations in the Eastern Caribbean, the Dominican Republic, Haiti, Mexico, Colombia, Venezuela, and Cuba. In the case of Cuba, he has managed this service for the past fourteen years. He has lived and worked in Latin America for over forty years.

He is a recipient of the Thomas Crowley Award for Outstanding Achievement.

Jay's university studies concentrated on international economics and Latin American affairs.

He received his bachelor of arts from the University of Florida and his master's from the School of Advanced International Studies of the Johns Hopkins University. He also studied at the Universidad de las Americas in Mexico. He has served on the Latin American Trade Committee of the US Department of Commerce.

At the University of Florida, he cooperated with the Center of Latin American Studies and is a Millennium participant for the Cuban Program. He is a founding member of the Cuban Studies Fund and serves on the Cuban Studies Program Advisory Group of the David Rockefeller Center at Harvard University.

Maria Conchita Mendez Piedra—Bio

Maria Conchita is a native of Cuba who immigrated to the United States in 1961. She is a descendant of "Mambises." Her great-grandfather, Coronel Segundo Corvison, served in the War of Independence. In 1939, he published a book, *En la Guerra y la Paz*, detailing the fabulous stories of the "Mambises." Maria Conchita is the director of Latin American Sales andTtrade Development for the Alabama State Port Authority. She has lived and traveled most of the Americas and has over thirty years' experience.

Her passion for Cuba came to fruition in 1975 while she was attending the University of Florida. She was one of the founders of *Areito*, a university publication.

Maria is a board member of La Mobile La Havana Society (the first sister city between Cuba and the United States) and cooperated with the Center for Latin American Studies University of Florida. She serves on the advisory board for the University of West Florida and was the founder and past president of the Hispanic American Business Association of the Gulf Coast, as well as an active participant in numerous forums in the United States and the Americas, including Cuba. She has received numerous awards in US-Cuba relations. She continues to be openly vocal on abolishing the embargo.

She was instrumental in facilitating contacts and opening doors for the first cargo shipments to Cuba.

Her heart never left Cuba. She continues to yearn for her homeland, *mi Cubita bella*.

Made in the USA
Middletown, DE
03 October 2016